Survival Strategies of the Gelatinous

Survival Strategies of the Gelatinous

INSIGHTS INTO JELLYFISH ECOLOGY

Alina Hazel

Mohammed Altaf Hussain

Contents

INDEX

Introduction

Jellyfish, those cryptic and ethereal animals that smoothly explore the huge breadths of the world's seas, have enraptured the interest of researchers, sea aficionados, and relaxed beachgoers the same. Their coagulated bodies, impelled by musical throbs, misrepresent a captivating environment formed by a long period of time of development. This investigation digs into the perplexing universe of jellyfish biology, unwinding the step by step processes for surviving that empower these organic entities to flourish in different marine conditions.

Developmental Stories of Coagulated Ability

Jellyfish, deductively named individuals from the phylum Cnidaria, have advanced exceptional variations that recognize them inside the embroidery of marine life. Their heredity follows back a huge number of years, giving a surprising excursion through Earth's developmental history.

The Development of Cnidarians

The transformative story of jellyfish starts with the development of Cnidarians, a different gathering that incorporates jellyfish as well as corals, ocean anemones, and hydrozoans. Cnidarians gloat particular stinging cells called cnidocytes, which assume an essential part in prey catch and protection.

Versatile Radiations:

Throughout transformative time, Cnidarians went through versatile radiations, enhancing into different structures to take advantage of a wide exhibit of natural specialties. This enhancement laid the preparation for the advancement of particular jellyfish species, each with its own arrangement of environmental variations.

Pelagic Ability: From Polyps to Medusae

The existence pattern of a jellyfish normally includes two principal organizes: the polyp and the medusa. Understanding the changes between these stages gives experiences into their methods for surviving.

Polyp Stage:

Jellyfish start their life as little polyps, appended to substrates like rocks or other hard surfaces. During this stage, they take part in agamic propagation, sprouting off new polyps that in the end form into mature medusae.

Medusa Stage:

The medusa stage, described by the natural chime molded body and following appendages, is the free-swimming period of the jellyfish life cycle. Medusae display exceptional variations for pelagic life, permitting them to explore flows and cover huge distances looking for prey and appropriate natural surroundings.

Transformative Weapons contest: Nematocysts and Prey Catch

One of the most characterizing elements of jellyfish is their capacity to catch prey utilizing particular stinging cells called nematocysts. These minuscule spear like designs are a demonstration of the transformative weapons contest among jellyfish and their prey.

Nematocyst System:

Nematocysts are snaked, cylindrical designs containing a spiked fiber. Upon contact with a potential prey thing, the nematocyst is set off to quickly release, infusing toxin and immobilizing the prey.

Prey Catch Systems:

Jellyfish utilize different systems for prey catch, from inactive floating to effectively beating their chimes to make water flows that bring prey into their appendages. A few animal groups show bioluminescence, drawing in prey in low-light circumstances.

The Dance of Variations: Biological Systems of Jellyfish

Jellyfish, with their assorted cluster of species, have developed a great collection of natural methodologies that empower them to get by as well as frequently flourish in the dynamic and some of the time testing states of marine environments.

Natural Resilience

Jellyfish exhibit an ability to strike to endure many ecological circumstances. From the bone chilling waters of polar districts to the warm, tropical oceans, jellyfish species display versatility that permits them to cross and flourish in assorted environments.

Temperature Varieties:

Some jellyfish species exhibit a serious level of resilience to temperature varieties. This versatility is especially important with regards to environmental change, where increasing ocean temperatures can impact the conveyance and overflow of marine life forms.

Saltiness Inclinations:

While jellyfish are ordinarily found in marine conditions, certain species can endure a scope of saltiness levels. This versatility permits them to possess estuaries and beach front regions where saltiness varies because of variables like stream spillover.

Conceptive Procedures

Jellyfish utilize a range of regenerative systems that add to their biological achievement. Their ability for both sexual and agamic generation improves their capacity to colonize and endure in different natural surroundings.

Mass Producing Occasions:

Numerous jellyfish species participate in mass generating occasions, where people discharge eggs and sperm into the water all the while. This synchronized regenerative technique expands the possibilities of fruitful preparation and the dispersal of hatchlings.

Polyp Industriousness:

The polyp phase of the jellyfish life cycle is in many cases described by an exceptional capacity to persevere in unfriendly circumstances. Polyps can endure ecological changes, permitting them to persevere through periods ominous for medusa endurance.

Specialty Extension and Sprout Elements

Jellyfish are known for their ability to frame sprouts, huge conglomerations of people that can have significant environmental effects. Understanding the elements driving blossom elements reveals insight into the procedures utilized by jellyfish to take advantage of natural specialties.

Pioneering Taking care of:

Jellyfish are pioneering feeders, consuming an assortment of prey, including zooplankton, little fish, and, surprisingly, other jellyfish. Their capacity to take advantage of an extensive variety of food sources adds to their progress in various marine conditions.

Sprout Triggers:

Different elements can set off jellyfish blossoms, including expanded supplement accessibility, temperature changes, and modifications in prey overflow. Blossoms address a methodology for quick populace increment, permitting jellyfish to benefit from good circumstances.

Vertical Relocations and Diel Examples

Jellyfish frequently show vertical relocations, traveling through the water section because of diel (day to day) designs. These relocations add to their scavenging techniques, hunter aversion, and conceptive ways of behaving.

Diel Vertical Relocation:

Numerous jellyfish species show diel vertical movement, pushing toward the surface around evening time to benefit from zooplankton pulled in by obscurity. During light hours, they might drop to more profound waters to keep away from predation.

Hunter Evasion:

Vertical movements act as a technique for hunter evasion, as jellyfish can take advantage of the front of haziness to take care of in surface waters while limiting openness to outwardly situated hunters.

Human-Jellyfish Communications: Difficulties and Conjunction

The complex dance among people and jellyfish isn't without challenges. Jellyfish stings, financial effects on fisheries and the travel industry, and ecological unsettling influences are features of the perplexing connection between these coagulated organic entities and the human world.

Stinging Episodes and Medical aid Measures

Jellyfish stings, brought about by the release of nematocysts, can bring about agony and uneasiness for people. Figuring out the components of stings and utilizing powerful medical aid measures are significant parts of moderating the effect of human-jellyfish associations.

Nematocyst Release:

The quick release of nematocysts upon contact with human skin prompts the infusion of toxin. Separating between jellyfish species, utilizing vinegar for specific stings, and eliminating appendages are key stages in emergency treatment.

Precaution Measures:

Forestalling jellyfish stings includes taking on methodologies like utilizing defensive apparel, remaining informed about neighborhood jellyfish species, and executing security estimates in traveler objections.

Monetary and Biological Effects

Jellyfish sprouts can significantly affect both the economy and the biology of seaside regions. From harming fishing stuff to discouraging sightseers, the outcomes of sprouts require extensive moderation and the executives methodologies.

Gear Harm and Functional Disturbances:

Jellyfish sprouts can prompt harm to fishing gear, causing functional disturbances and monetary misfortunes for fishing networks. Moderating these effects requires economical fisheries the board rehearses.

Security Worries for Sightseers:

The travel industry subordinate seaside networks face financial difficulties when security concerns connected with jellyfish stings prevent guests. Supportable the travel industry practices and public mindfulness drives are fundamental for encouraging concurrence.

Moderation and The executives Procedures

Moderating the effect of jellyfish sprouts requires a mix of natural preservation, practical fisheries the executives, mechanical developments, and local area based drives. Understanding the harmony between human exercises and environmental elements is central for effective conjunction.

Biological system Based Administration:

Taking on environment based administration approaches recognizes the interconnectedness of marine biological systems. Protecting basic territories, reestablishing corrupted conditions, and taking into account the job of jellyfish in more extensive biological settings are fundamental parts.

Feasible Fisheries The board:

Executing maintainable fisheries the executives rehearses includes controlling fishing exercises, laying out get restricts, and safeguarding basic natural surroundings. Adjusting the requirements of fisheries with the conservation of environment wellbeing is essential for maintainable asset use.

Mechanical Developments:

Saddling trend setting innovations like early admonition frameworks, remote detecting, and submerged mechanical technology upgrades our capacity to screen and answer jellyfish elements. Biocontrol measures and hereditary change research address inventive ways to deal with jellyfish the board.

Local area Based Drives:

Connecting with nearby networks and people in general in jellyfish mindfulness, training, and checking drives cultivates a feeling of shared liability. Supportable the travel industry rehearses, resident science programs, and instructive effort add to dependable communications with marine conditions.

Unwinding the Secrets: Future Bearings in Jellyfish Biology

As we keep on revealing the complexities of jellyfish environment, various inquiries and roads for investigation entice mainstream researchers. From the sub-atomic instruments of nematocyst release to the more extensive ramifications of environmental change on jellyfish elements, what's in store guarantees a more profound comprehension of these coagulated wonders.

Sub-atomic Bits of knowledge into Nematocyst Capability

Opening the atomic mysteries of nematocyst capability offers expected applications in medication, biotechnology, and materials science. Understanding the instruments behind nematocyst release and toxin piece might make ready for developments motivated by jellyfish science.

Environmental Change and Jellyfish Elements

The effects of environmental change on sea temperatures, flows, and supplement accessibility have extensive ramifications for jellyfish biology. Examination into the particular reactions of jellyfish species to environment related changes gives important bits of knowledge into future biological situations.

Preservation Methodologies for Weak Species

While some jellyfish species flourish in different conditions, others face dangers from environment corruption, contamination, and overfishing. Creating protection techniques for weak jellyfish species adds to the general wellbeing and variety of marine environments.

Economical Hydroponics and Jellyfish Biomass Usage

Investigating the capability of jellyfish in supportable hydroponics and biomass usage presents open doors for both biological and monetary advantages. Investigation into the possibility of jellyfish hydroponics and the improvement of significant worth added items can add to food security and ecological supportability.

Public Commitment and Mindful The travel industry

Reinforcing public commitment and advancing capable the travel industry rehearses are progressing difficulties in overseeing human-jellyfish cooperations. Imaginative methodologies, for example, computer generated reality encounters and intuitive instructive stages, can upgrade public mindfulness and interest.

1. **Definition and Characteristics of Jellyfish**

   Jellyfish, with their smooth throbbing chimes and following limbs, address an entrancing and mysterious domain inside the immense breadth of the world's seas. These coagulated animals, officially known as medusae, have a place with the phylum Cnidaria and display remarkable qualities that put them aside in the embroidery of marine life. This investigation dives into the definition and key attributes of jellyfish, unwinding the secrets of their life structures, life cycle, and environmental jobs.

Characterizing Jellyfish

Ordered Grouping

Jellyfish have a place with the phylum Cnidaria, which incorporates a different cluster of marine creatures like corals, ocean anemones, and hydroids. Inside Cnidaria, jellyfish are additionally characterized into the class Scyphozoa (genuine jellyfish), Cubozoa (box jellyfish), Staurozoa (followed jellyfish), and Hydrozoa (hydrozoans, which remember some jellyfish species for their life cycle).

Thick Design

The expression "jellyfish" is gotten from the coagulated idea of these animals. Their bodies are made principally out of water (roughly 95%), giving them a clear and sensitive appearance. The coagulated substance gives lightness, permitting jellyfish to drift and move easily through the water.

Key Attributes of Jellyfish

Spiral Evenness

One of the principal traits of jellyfish is their spiral evenness. Spiral evenness implies that the body parts are organized around a focal hub, similar as the spokes of a wheel. This balance permits jellyfish to move smoothly toward any path, making them very much adjusted to a pelagic (vast ocean) way of life.

Mesoglea: The Thick Lattice

The mesoglea, the jam like substance that makes up the heft of a jellyfish's body, is an exceptional component. This clear framework offers underlying help and lightness, permitting jellyfish to keep up with their ringer formed structure. The mesoglea likewise goes about as a repository for supplements.

Nematocysts: Particular Stinging Cells

Maybe one of the most famous elements of jellyfish is the presence of particular stinging cells called nematocysts. Nematocysts are tiny spear like designs situated on the appendages. They assume an essential part in catching prey and shielding against expected dangers.

Prey Catch Component:

At the point when a jellyfish comes into contact with prey, nematocysts violently release, infusing toxin into the objective. This immobilizes or kills the prey, and the jellyfish's arms then, at that point, transport it to the life form's focal mouth.

Fluctuated Nematocyst Types:

Various types of jellyfish have nematocysts with fluctuating designs and works. Some are adjusted for prey catch, while others are utilized for safeguard against hunters. The variety of nematocyst types mirrors the versatility of jellyfish to various environmental specialties.

Ringer or Medusa Structure

Jellyfish display an unmistakable body structure known as the medusa or ringer. This chime molded structure permits jellyfish to impel themselves through the water by cadenced withdrawals. The ringer contains the focal mouth and stomach related framework, as well as expansions known as oral arms.

Headway:

The throbbing movement of the ringer pushes jellyfish forward, and they can likewise move upward by changing the course of their throbs. This ringer structure is a critical variation for life in the untamed sea.

Oral Arms:

Encompassing the mouth, jellyfish frequently have long, meaty designs called oral arms. These arms help in the taking care of and assimilation of prey. The oral arms can shift in number and construction among various jellyfish species.

Limbs and Prey Catch

Jellyfish have long, following limbs furnished with nematocysts. These arms fill various needs, including prey catch, protection against hunters, and material detecting. The limbs are a urgent part of the complex taking care of techniques utilized by jellyfish.

Arm Capability:

Limbs broaden outward from the chime and make a floating drape of stinging cells. As jellyfish travel through the water, the arms limp along, catching prey that comes into contact with the nematocysts.

Variable Length and Thickness:

The length and thickness of appendages change among jellyfish species. Some have short and thickly stuffed arms, while others have long, following strands. These varieties are transformations to the particular environmental specialties and prey kinds of various jellyfish.

Life Cycle: Polyp and Medusa Stages

The existence pattern of a jellyfish regularly includes two fundamental stages: the polyp and the medusa. This variation of ages is a typical component in the existence patterns of numerous cnidarians.

Polyp Stage:

Jellyfish start their life as polyps, joined to a substrate in marine conditions. During the polyp stage, agamic multiplication happens through sprouting, bringing about adolescent medusae. Polyps are much of the time unnoticeable and less versatile than the medusa stage.

Medusa Stage:

The medusa stage addresses the free-swimming stage described by the chime formed body. Medusae are the more unmistakable type of jellyfish and are answerable for exercises like taking care of, generation, and answering ecological upgrades.

Bioluminescence

A few types of jellyfish display bioluminescence, an interesting peculiarity where they produce light. Bioluminescence is remembered to fill various needs, including drawing in prey, dissuading hunters, and correspondence inside the species.

Natural Importance:

In obscurity profundities of the sea, bioluminescence turns into an essential transformation. Jellyfish utilize their capacity to produce light to explore, impart, and participate in different ways of behaving that add to their endurance.

Correspondence:

Bioluminescence assumes a part in intraspecific correspondence among jellyfish. Blazing examples and varieties are utilized to pass messages related on to mating, an area, and other social collaborations.

Natural Variations

Jellyfish feature noteworthy transformations to different natural circumstances. From temperature varieties to saltiness inclinations, their capacity to flourish in a scope of environments adds to their worldwide circulation.

Temperature Resilience:

Some jellyfish species show a serious level of temperature resilience, permitting them to possess both polar and tropical waters. Their capacity to conform to various warm circumstances is a demonstration of their natural adaptability.

Saltiness Inclinations:

While jellyfish are normally found in marine conditions, certain species can endure a scope of saltiness levels. This flexibility empowers them to possess estuaries and beach front regions where saltiness might vacillate.

2. **Importance of Understanding Jellyfish Ecology**

Jellyfish, with their elegant undulations and clear bodies, possess the strange domains of the world's seas, enamoring the creative mind of researchers, hippies, and the overall population. Past their tasteful allure, understanding the complexities of jellyfish environment is of central significance. This investigation dives into the meaning of grasping jellyfish biology, looking at their parts in marine biological systems, the difficulties they present, and the more extensive ramifications for ecological protection and human prosperity.

1. **Environment Availability and Equilibrium**

   1.1. Cornerstone Species and Trophic Communications

   Jellyfish, in spite of their apparently basic life structures, frequently assume essential parts as cornerstone species in marine biological systems. Their communications with different creatures, especially with regards to trophic elements, can significantly affect environment construction and capability.

   1.1.1. Hunter Prey Connections:

Jellyfish are the two hunters and prey, participating in complex cooperations with different marine living beings. A few types of jellyfish feed on zooplankton, little fish, and, surprisingly, other jellyfish, impacting the overflow of these prey populaces. On the other hand, jellyfish act as prey for species, for example, ocean turtles and certain fish, adding to the perplexing trap of hunter prey connections.

1.1.2. Fisheries Elements:

Understanding the job of jellyfish in fisheries elements is significant for economical asset the executives. Now and again, jellyfish sprouts can rival fish for food assets or harm fishing gear. On the other hand, certain fish species benefit from the presence of jellyfish as a food source. Adjusting these connections is fundamental for keeping up with sound fish populaces and reasonable fisheries.

1.2. Supplement Cycling and Marine Efficiency

Jellyfish add to supplement pushing in marine biological systems through their taking care of and discharge processes. As they drink prey, jellyfish discharge supplements once more into the water as waste. This supplement advancement can animate phytoplankton development, impacting essential efficiency in the sea.

1.2.1. Organic Siphon:

The natural siphon, a vital part of marine biological systems, includes the exchange of carbon from the environment to the profound sea through the sinking of natural matter. Jellyfish, by affecting the overflow of phytoplankton, can by implication influence the proficiency of the natural siphon. Understanding these elements is pivotal for grasping the more extensive carbon cycling in the seas.

1.2.2. Effect on Phytoplankton Sprouts:

Some jellyfish species display taking care of ways of behaving that target explicit kinds of phytoplankton. By specifically consuming specific phytoplankton, jellyfish can impact the piece of phytoplankton networks and the event of blossoms. These elements have suggestions for the general efficiency and soundness of marine biological systems.

2. Natural Markers and Environmental Change

2.1. Aversion to Natural Changes

Jellyfish are touchy marks of ecological changes, making them important sentinels for surveying the wellbeing of marine biological systems. Different parts of jellyfish biology, including their appropriation, overflow, and regenerative examples, can be affected by shifts in natural circumstances.

2.1.1. Temperature and Environment:

The circulation and conduct of jellyfish are firmly connected to the ocean temperature. As worldwide temperatures climb because of environmental change, jellyfish populaces might answer by moving their reaches or modifying their overflow. Checking these progressions gives bits of knowledge into the more extensive effects of environmental change on marine biodiversity.

2.1.2. Sea Fermentation:

The continuous course of sea fermentation, driven by the assimilation of overabundance carbon dioxide via seawater, can influence the turn of events and physiology of jellyfish. Understanding how jellyfish answer changing sea science adds as far as anyone is concerned of the outcomes of anthropogenic fossil fuel byproducts.

2.2. Biogeographical Movements

Noticing changes in the conveyance and overflow of jellyfish can show more extensive biogeographical changes in marine biological systems. Such moves might have flowing consequences for the arrangement of marine networks and the general design of maritime food networks.

2.2.1. Intrusive Species Elements:

Certain jellyfish species can become obtrusive in new areas, with human exercises, for example, delivering adding to their spread. The foundation of intrusive jellyfish can upset neighborhood biological systems, outcompeting local species and influencing fisheries. Concentrating on these elements helps with creating procedures for the avoidance and the board of obtrusive species.

2.2.2. Biodiversity Areas of interest and Protection Needs:

Distinguishing regions where jellyfish variety is especially high can act as a mark of biodiversity areas of interest. These districts might require unique preservation consideration regarding save the complicated cooperations and natural jobs played by different jellyfish species.

3. **Human-Jellyfish Cooperations and Financial Effects**

3.1. The travel industry and Amusement

Jellyfish connections with people, whether through the travel industry or sporting exercises, convey the two dangers and open doors. Understanding the environmental drivers of jellyfish overflow and conduct is fundamental for overseeing and relieving expected adverse consequences on the travel industry.

3.1.1. Stinging Occurrences:

Jellyfish stings can represent a danger to beachgoers and travelers. Information on jellyfish environment, including factors affecting the recurrence and seriousness of stinging occurrences, illuminates security measures and medical aid conventions. Public mindfulness crusades are fundamental for teaching networks and guests about the dangers related with jellyfish experiences.

3.1.2. Jellyfish Blossoms and The travel industry Effect:

Blossoms of specific jellyfish species can affect the travel industry by discouraging guests from participating in water-based exercises. Understanding the circumstances that lead to jellyfish blossoms empowers specialists to carry out checking frameworks and give ideal data to vacationers, limiting disturbances to neighborhood economies.

3.2. Fisheries and Hydroponics

Jellyfish can have complex collaborations with fisheries and hydroponics tasks, affecting both fish stocks and the productivity of these ventures. Perceiving the environmental jobs of jellyfish helps in contriving systems for reasonable fisheries the executives.

3.2.1. Serious Cooperations with Fish:

Now and again, jellyfish sprouts might rival fish for food assets. This opposition can influence fish development rates and generally speaking fishery yields. Understanding the biological elements among jellyfish and fish species directs the improvement of procedures to moderate expected adverse consequences on fisheries.

3.2.2. Hydroponics Difficulties:

Jellyfish can present difficulties to hydroponics tasks by obstructing admission pipes, harming nets, or outcompeting cultivated species for food. Concentrating on the biological collaborations among jellyfish and hydroponics frameworks is imperative for planning versatile and reasonable hydroponics rehearses.

4. Moderation and The board Systems

4.1. Environment Based Administration

Understanding jellyfish nature is crucial to taking on biological system based administration draws near. Safeguarding basic living spaces, overseeing fisheries economically, and taking into account the more extensive natural setting are key parts of alleviating and dealing with the effects of jellyfish on marine environments.

4.1.1. Marine Safeguarded Regions:

Laying out marine safeguarded regions (MPAs) helps preserve basic environments and shield weak species from the effects of human exercises. MPAs add to the versatility of marine biological systems, guaranteeing that the natural jobs of jellyfish and different life forms are protected.

4.1.2. Reclamation Drives:

Endeavors to reestablish debased marine natural surroundings add to the general strength of biological systems. Reclamation drives improve the flexibility of biological systems to natural changes, diminishing the defenselessness of marine networks to interruptions brought about by elements, for example, overfishing and territory annihilation.

4.2. Practical Fisheries The board

Alleviating the effect of jellyfish on fisheries includes carrying out maintainable fisheries the executives rehearses. Guideline of fishing exercises, foundation of catch cutoff points, and security of basic territories are fundamental parts of keeping a harmony among fisheries and the more extensive marine climate.

4.2.1. Incorporated Administration Plans:

Creating incorporated administration designs that consider the collaborations among jellyfish and fish species is urgent. Such plans address the biological jobs of jellyfish in marine environments, going for the gold conjunction among fisheries and the common habitat.

4.2.2. Mechanical Developments:

Tackling cutting edge innovations, like early admonition frameworks, remote detecting, and submerged mechanical technology, improves our capacity to screen and answer jellyfish elements. Imaginative arrangements, including bio-control measures and hereditary change research, address likely roads for economical fisheries the executives.

4.3. Local area Commitment and Training

Drawing in neighborhood networks and the general population in jellyfish mindfulness, training, and checking drives cultivates a feeling of shared liability. Reasonable the travel industry rehearses, resident science programs, and instructive effort add to mindful associations with marine conditions.

4.3.1. Public Mindfulness Missions:

Instructive missions assume an imperative part in illuminating people in general about jellyfish environment, the dangers related with stinging episodes, and the significance of mindful the travel industry rehearses. Engaging people group with information upgrades their capacity to coincide with jellyfish and add to protection endeavors.

4.3.2. Resident Science Projects:

Including general society in resident science programs permits people to contribute significant information on jellyfish populaces and conduct. Resident science drives make a feeling of stewardship and natural obligation, encouraging a cooperative way to deal with understanding and monitoring marine biological systems.

5. Research Wildernesses and Future Headings

5.1. Sub-atomic Experiences into Jellyfish Science

Propelling comprehension we might interpret jellyfish environment includes digging into sub-atomic bits of knowledge, especially with respect to nematocyst capability, toxin creation, and hereditary variations. These atomic examinations offer possible applications in medication, biotechnology, and materials science.

5.1.1. Biomedical Applications:

Concentrating on the sub-atomic instruments behind nematocyst release and toxin creation might prompt revelations with biomedical applications. The special properties of jellyfish poisons, for instance, have been investigated for their possible in creating drugs and clinical medicines.

5.1.2. Biotechnology and Materials Science:

The striking properties of jellyfish, including their coagulated lattice and particular cells, motivate advancements in biotechnology and materials science. Understanding the atomic premise of these elements opens roads for creating bio-motivated materials and advancements.

5.2. Environmental Change and Jellyfish Elements

Environmental change presents critical difficulties to marine biological systems, and understanding how jellyfish answer changing ecological circumstances is pivotal. Examination into the particular reactions of jellyfish species to environment related changes gives significant bits of knowledge into future biological situations.

5.2.1. Appropriation Movements and Living space Changes:

Checking shifts in the dissemination of jellyfish species and their reactions to environment changes adds to how we might interpret environmental change influences on marine biodiversity. Such exploration illuminates forecasts about the possible development or constriction of jellyfish populaces in various districts.

5.2.2. Sea Fermentation Studies:

Examining how jellyfish answer sea fermentation upgrades how we might interpret the physiological impacts of changing seawater science. These examinations add to more extensive endeavors to relieve the effects of sea fermentation on marine life forms.

5.3. Protection Procedures for Weak Species

While some jellyfish species flourish in different conditions, others face dangers from territory debasement, contamination, and overfishing. Creating protection systems for weak jellyfish species adds to the general wellbeing and variety of marine environments.

5.3.1. Natural surroundings Insurance and Rebuilding:

Distinguishing and safeguarding basic environments for weak jellyfish species is fundamental for their protection. Reclamation drives, pointed toward restoring debased territories, add to the versatility of these environments.

5.3.2. Incorporated Preservation Plans:

Incorporating jellyfish preservation into more extensive marine protection plans guarantees a comprehensive methodology. Protection methodologies ought to consider the interconnectedness of marine environments and the jobs played by various species, including jellyfish, in keeping up with natural equilibrium.

5.4. Economical Hydroponics and Biomass Usage

Investigating the capability of jellyfish in manageable hydroponics and biomass usage presents valuable open doors for both biological and financial advantages. Investigation into the achievability of jellyfish hydroponics and the improvement of significant worth added items can add to food security and natural manageability.

5.4.1. Hydroponics Developments:

Examining the capability of jellyfish in hydroponics requires imaginative ways to deal with address difficulties like food transformation effectiveness, natural effect, and market agreeableness. Supportable hydroponics rehearses that coordinate jellyfish development with other marine assets hold guarantee for satisfying future food needs.

5.4.2. Biomass Usage and Roundabout Economy:

Investigating ways of using jellyfish biomass in different enterprises, like farming and biotechnology, adds to the improvement of a round economy. Finding esteem in jellyfish results can lessen squander and set out open doors for supportable asset usage.

C. Overview of the Book's Focus on Survival Strategies

Inside the huge region of marine environments, jellyfish arise as confounding occupants, enthralling specialists, researchers, and nature devotees the same. This book leaves on a thorough investigation of jellyfish environment, digging into their step by step processes for surviving, social variations, and biological jobs that shape their reality on the planet's seas. As we unwind the secrets of jellyfish endurance, this outline gives a guide, featuring key subjects and parts that structure the foundation of our investigation.

Characterizing Jellyfish - Life structures, Order, and Advancement

The excursion starts with a profound plunge into the basic parts of jellyfish. This section offers an extensive outline of their life structures, order inside the phylum Cnidaria, and the developmental achievements that have molded their exceptional qualities. Understanding the structure blocks of jellyfish science makes way for unwinding the complexities of their methods for surviving.

Life Cycle Elements - Polyp to Medusa Transformation

The existence pattern of jellyfish unfurls in a captivating dance among polyp and medusa stages. This section investigates the transformation from polyp to medusa, enumerating the conceptive techniques, agamic propagation through growing, and the natural meaning of every life stage. By following the formative excursion of jellyfish, we gain experiences into the versatile methodologies that guarantee their coherence in different marine conditions.

Detecting the Climate - Material Reactions and Route

Endurance in the powerful universe of the sea requests intense tangible abilities. This part centers around how jellyfish sense and answer their current circumstance. From material reactions to ecological signs, the many-sided systems that guide jellyfish route and conduct become exposed. Understanding these tangible transformations gives a brief look into the techniques that empower jellyfish to flourish in the midst of consistently changing maritime circumstances.

Prey Catch and Taking care of Methodologies - Nematocysts and Then some

Integral to the endurance of jellyfish is their capacity to proficiently catch prey. Part 4 digs into the complex weaponry of jellyfish - the nematocysts. Past the stinging cells, we investigate the assorted taking care of systems utilized by various jellyfish species. From channel taking care of to effectively hunting prey, this section uncovers the multi-layered approaches that add to their prosperity as hunters in marine environments.

Natural Variations - Temperature, Saltiness, and Then some

Getting through in different marine environments requires versatility. Part 5 explores how jellyfish explore a scope of ecological circumstances. From temperature resilience to saltiness inclinations, the conversation unfurls the exceptional flexibility of jellyfish. This versatility shapes their appropriation as well as positions them as strong players notwithstanding natural inconstancy.

Bioluminescence and Correspondence - Enlightening the Profundities

Jellyfish, with their ethereal shine, utilize bioluminescence for different purposes.

Section 6 investigates the meaning of bioluminescence in jellyfish environment. Past its stylish allure, we uncover how jellyfish utilize light outflow for correspondence inside their species, exploring the dim profundities of the sea, and possibly stopping hunters.

Collaborations with Different Species - Biological Jobs and Organizations

Endurance in marine environments is unpredictably connected to associations with different species. Section 7 reveals insight into the natural jobs of jellyfish and their associations with different marine organic entities. From advantageous connections to hunter prey elements, understanding these communications enhances our cognizance of jellyfish as vital parts of intricate marine environments.

Guard Instruments - Adapting to Hunters and Dangers

In the complicated dance of endurance, guard systems assume a urgent part. Section 8 spotlights on how jellyfish adapt to hunters and expected dangers. From mysterious ways of behaving to venomous hindrances, we disentangle the procedures that empower jellyfish to explore the difficulties presented by their regular foes and natural stressors.

Effect on Biological systems - Natural Outcomes of Jellyfish Sprouts

Step by step processes for surviving frequently have more extensive environmental results. Section 9 analyzes the effect of jellyfish on marine environments, especially with regards to sprouts. Understanding how jellyfish impact supplement cycling, essential efficiency, and trophic elements gives experiences into their jobs as both forces to be reckoned with and responders to ecological changes.

Human-Jellyfish Associations - Difficulties and Valuable open doors

As human exercises cross with marine conditions, Part 10 investigates the difficulties and potential open doors introduced by human-jellyfish connections. From security worries for vacationers to the monetary effects on fisheries and the travel industry, this part explores the fragile equilibrium expected for conjunction among people and jellyfish.

Alleviation and The board Procedures - Adjusting Human and Natural Requirements

In the journey for maintainable conjunction, Section 11 dives into moderation and the board techniques. From environment based ways to deal with maintainable fisheries the board, this section frames the actions expected to offset human requirements with biological preservation. Mechanical advancements, local area commitment, and public mindfulness drives highlight unmistakably in the conversation.

Future Headings in Jellyfish Nature - Unwinding the Secrets

The closing part looks into the future, featuring roads for additional investigation in jellyfish nature. From sub-atomic bits of knowledge into nematocyst capability to the ramifications of environmental change on jellyfish elements, the guide unfurls with questions and potential leap forwards that guarantee a more profound comprehension of these thick wonders.

Chapter 1

The World Of Jellyfish

The hypnotizing domain of jellyfish is a dazzling and secretive part of marine life that has fascinated researchers, scientists, and nature lovers for quite a long time. These coagulated animals, with their clear bodies and elegant developments, occupy seas around the world, going from the shallow waterfront waters to the most unfathomable pit. In this investigation of the universe of jellyfish, we dig into their one of a kind qualities, natural importance, various species, and the complicated equilibrium they keep up with inside marine environments.

Life systems and Transformations:

Jellyfish, logically known as jams or medusae, have a place with the phylum Cnidaria. Their oversimplified at this point exquisite body structure is described by a thick chime molded umbrella and following limbs furnished with specific stinging cells called nematocysts. These nematocysts assume a urgent part in catching prey and hindering possible hunters. The umbrella throbs help in movement, pushing the jellyfish through the water with a powerful elegance.

One of the most interesting variations of jellyfish is their capacity to go through two unmistakable life stages - the medusa and the polyp. This perplexing life cycle permits them to explore different natural difficulties and expand their possibilities of endurance.

Biodiversity of Jellyfish:

The universe of jellyfish brags a surprising variety species, running in size from minute, almost imperceptible animals to epic monsters that can equal the components of a human. Among the notable species are the moon jellyfish (Aurelia aurita), box jellyfish (Chironex fleckeri), and lion's mane jellyfish (Cyanea capillata). Every species displays remarkable attributes, from the hypnotizing bioluminescence of specific remote ocean jellyfish to the venomous appendages of others.

Jellyfish flourish in various oceanic conditions, adjusting to conditions going from tropical coral reefs to bone chilling polar waters. Their flexibility and strength make them a central member in the unpredictable embroidery of marine environments.

Natural Significance:

Regardless of their fragile appearance, jellyfish assume a fundamental part in keeping up with the natural equilibrium of the seas. As deft hunters, they assist with controlling the number of inhabitants in tiny fish, little fish, and shellfish. By forestalling the uncontrolled expansion of these organic entities, jellyfish by implication impact the soundness of whole marine food networks.

Besides, jellyfish act as both prey and hunter, shaping a fundamental connection in the marine pecking order. Ocean turtles, sunfish, and certain types of fish depend on jellyfish as a huge food source, while bigger jellyfish feed on more modest planktonic organic entities. The perplexing connections among jellyfish and other marine species feature their significance in supporting maritime biodiversity.

Blossom Peculiarity:

Jellyfish blossoms, portrayed by the unexpected and productive expansion in jellyfish populaces, are a characteristic peculiarity that can have huge environmental results. While these sprouts are a normal piece of jellyfish life cycles, anthropogenic factors, for example, overfishing, contamination, and environmental change have prompted an expansion in their recurrence and power.

Huge jellyfish sprouts can disturb fisheries, obstruct power plant admissions, and effect neighborhood economies. The complicated transaction between ecological elements and jellyfish elements highlights the requirement for a superior comprehension of these puzzling animals to relieve expected adverse consequences on human exercises and marine environments.

Bioluminescence and Correspondence:

Jellyfish are famous for their dazzling bioluminescent presentations, a hypnotizing light show delivered by particular cells inside their bodies. This bioluminescence fills different needs, including drawing in prey, deflecting hunters, and working with correspondence among individuals from similar species.

Specialists have found that jellyfish convey utilizing light motions toward coordinate gathering developments, mating ceremonies, and reactions to ecological upgrades. Unwinding the complexities of jellyfish correspondence reveals insight on their social ways of behaving as well as on the more extensive comprehension of correspondence components in the immense, to a great extent neglected profundities of the sea.

Human Communication and Effect:

While jellyfish satisfy fundamental biological jobs, their connections with people can have both positive and pessimistic results. The venomous stings of specific species represent a danger to swimmers, making it essential for waterfront networks to execute viable wellbeing measures. Simultaneously, jellyfish-based items, for example, collagen extricated from their bodies, have tracked down applications in clinical exploration and corrective businesses.

Anthropogenic elements, including environmental change, overfishing, and beach front turn of events, add to the mind boggling elements among jellyfish and human exercises. Understanding and dealing with these cooperations are fundamental for the economical conjunction of people and jellyfish in shared beach front conditions.

Preservation and Future Viewpoints:

Given the rising recurrence of jellyfish blossoms and their likely effect on biological systems and human exercises, the protection of these marine animals has turned into a squeezing concern. Creating techniques to alleviate the variables adding to jellyfish populace blasts, for example, diminishing supplement overflow and tending to environmental change, is essential for keeping up with the fragile equilibrium of marine biological systems.

Headways in sea life science and innovation offer new roads for concentrating on jellyfish and their environments. Independent submerged vehicles, remote detecting advancements, and atomic science methods empower analysts to investigate the profundities of the sea and unwind the secrets of jellyfish science, conduct, and biology.

1.1 Classification and Diversity of Jellyfish Species

The seas, immense and overflowing with life, are home to a phenomenal exhibit of animals, each possessing a particular specialty in the complex embroidery of marine environments. Among these, jellyfish stand apart as entrancing and cryptic occupants, displaying a wonderful variety of structures, ways of behaving, and transformations. This far reaching investigation plans to dig into the characterization and variety of jellyfish species, revealing insight into the many-sided ordered connections and the horde variations that have permitted these coagulated living beings to flourish in different oceanic conditions.

Scientific classification of Jellyfish:

The scientific classification of jellyfish, officially known as Scyphozoa, Cubozoa, and Hydrozoa, mirrors the developmental connections and particular qualities that characterize each gathering. Understanding the ordered progressive system gives an establishment to investigating the gigantic variety inside the universe of jellyfish.

1.1. Class Scyphozoa:

Class Scyphozoa includes the genuine jellyfish, unmistakable by their chime formed medusae and stinging limbs. This class is additionally separated into requests, families, and genera in light of morphological highlights and hereditary examinations. Remarkable models incorporate the moon jellyfish (Aurelia aurita) and the lion's mane jellyfish (Cyanea capillata).

1.2. Class Cubozoa:

Cubozoans, ordinarily known as box jellyfish, are portrayed by their block formed medusae and strong toxin. This class incorporates the absolute most venomous jellyfish species, for example, Chironex fleckeri. The scientific classification of Cubozoa is coordinated into requests, families, and genera, mirroring the variety inside this gathering.

1.3. Class Hydrozoa:

Hydrozoans incorporate an extensive variety of jellyfish species, including both pilgrim and lone structures. Dissimilar to the bigger and more prominent Scyphozoa and

Cubozoa, hydrozoans frequently have more modest medusae and a complicated life cycle including polyp and medusa stages. The ordered characterization of Hydrozoa incorporates orders like Anthoathecata and Leptothecata, featuring the variety inside this class.

Morphological Variety:

The morphological variety of jellyfish species is a demonstration of their capacity to adjust to different marine conditions. Looking at the unmistakable elements of various species gives important experiences into their developmental history and natural jobs.

2.1. Chime Shape and Size:

Jellyfish show an extensive variety of ringer shapes and sizes, from the sensitive, straightforward chimes of little species to the vigorous and forcing designs of bigger ones. The chime fills in as the focal center point for headway, lodging essential organs and working with throbs that drive the jellyfish through the water. The variety in size and shape reflects variations to explicit biological specialties and ecological circumstances.

2.2. Arm Plan and Capability:

Limbs are a characterizing component of jellyfish, furnished with specific stinging cells called nematocysts. The course of action, length, and thickness of limbs change among species, impacting their taking care of procedures and associations with prey. Some jellyfish have long, following limbs that catch prey from a good ways, while others have more limited appendages appropriate for tight situation hunting.

2.3. Bioluminescence:

Bioluminescence, the creation of light by living creatures, is a momentous component shown by specific jellyfish species. Bioluminescent jellyfish utilize light as a device for correspondence, predation, and protection. The variety of bioluminescent examples and tones among jellyfish species mirrors their complicated flagging components and natural jobs in obscurity profundities of the sea.

Geographic Appropriation and Living space Inclinations:

Jellyfish species exhibit a noteworthy flexibility to different marine territories, from the surface waters of tropical oceans to the bone chilling profundities of polar seas. Understanding their geographic appropriation and living space inclinations gives important experiences into the variables impacting their advancement and biological jobs.

3.1. Pelagic and Benthic Conditions:

While some jellyfish species occupy the untamed sea, known as pelagic species, others incline toward benthic conditions, staying close to the sea depths. The transformation to either pelagic or benthic ways of life is affected by elements like prey accessibility, temperature, and flows. This different dissemination permits jellyfish to possess many natural specialties.

3.2. Beach front and Remote ocean Natural surroundings:

Jellyfish are ordinarily tracked down in seaside waters, where supplement rich flows support bountiful prey. Furthermore, certain species have adjusted to the outrageous states of the remote ocean, displaying exceptional morphological and physiological highlights that empower them to make due exposed, dull pit.

Remarkable Jellyfish Species:

Inside the huge range of jellyfish variety, a few animal types have acquired unmistakable quality because of their exceptional attributes, natural importance, or, at times, their effect on human exercises. Investigating the elements of these prominent species gives a more profound comprehension of the broadness of jellyfish variety.

4.1. Moon Jellyfish (Aurelia aurita):

The moon jellyfish is one of the most conspicuous and generally concentrated on jellyfish species. With its clear chime and fragile appearance, Aurelia aurita is much of the time tracked down in beach front waters and is known for its delicate throbbing developments. Notwithstanding its apparently harmless nature, this species assumes a vital part in marine environments by controlling the overflow of little prey organic entities.

4.2. Box Jellyfish (Chironex fleckeri):

Box jellyfish, having a place with the class Cubozoa, are notorious for their powerful toxin and block molded chimes. Chironex fleckeri, tracked down in the waters of the Indo-Pacific district, is viewed as quite possibly of the most venomous marine animal. Their mind boggling eyes and high level sensory system put them aside from other jellyfish, featuring the variety inside the class Cubozoa.

4.3. Lion's Mane Jellyfish (Cyanea capillata):

The lion's mane jellyfish, with its noteworthy exhibit of long, streaming appendages, is the biggest known jellyfish species. Found in cool northern and cold waters, Cyanea capillata shows a striking appearance and is an unquenchable hunter. Understanding the environmental jobs of such huge jellyfish species adds as far as anyone is concerned of marine food networks and supplement cycling.

4.4. Turritopsis dohrnii (The Godlike Jellyfish):

Turritopsis dohrnii, frequently alluded to as the "godlike jellyfish," has acquired consideration for its remarkable capacity to return its cells to a previous formative stage, actually turning around the maturing system. This striking natural peculiarity permits the jellyfish to possibly live endlessly. The investigation of Turritopsis dohrnii has suggestions for figuring out the cycles of maturing and recovery in different creatures.

Life Cycle and Proliferation:

The existence pattern of jellyfish is a complicated and captivating cycle that includes both sexual and abiogenetic propagation. Understanding the complexities of their conceptive procedures gives bits of knowledge into their environmental achievement and flexibility.

5.1. Polyp and Medusa Stages:

Jellyfish display a metagenetic life cycle, switching back and forth among polyp and medusa stages. The polyp, a sessile and frequently provincial structure, goes through agamic propagation through sprouting to create youthful medusae. These medusae, thus, form into mature people fit for sexual propagation. This double life stage technique permits jellyfish to take advantage of various biological specialties and natural circumstances.

5.2. Sexual Proliferation:

Sexual propagation in jellyfish includes the arrival of gametes (sperm and eggs) into the water, where treatment happens. The subsequent planula hatchlings choose a substrate and form into polyps, starting the abiogenetic period of the existence cycle. The harmony among sexual and abiogenetic proliferation adds to the populace elements and flexibility of jellyfish species.

Natural Difficulties and Protection:

Jellyfish, in spite of their natural importance, face various difficulties in the cutting edge period, generally ascribed to human exercises and ecological changes. Examining the effect of these difficulties on jellyfish populaces is critical for creating viable protection systems.

6.1. Environmental Change and Sea Fermentation:

Environmental change and the related climb in ocean temperatures significantly affect marine biological systems, impacting the appropriation and overflow of jellyfish species. Furthermore, sea fermentation, an outcome of expanded carbon dioxide retention via seawater, can influence the calcareous designs of jellyfish and their prey. Understanding the reactions of jellyfish to these natural changes is fundamental for anticipating their future overflow and dissemination.

6.2. Overfishing and Fisheries Communications:

Overfishing can disturb marine food networks and make conditions ideal for jellyfish blossoms. Certain jellyfish species flourish in conditions where their regular hunters, for example, huge fish and ocean turtles, have been exhausted by overfishing. The connections among jellyfish and fisheries highlight the requirement for supportable fishing practices to keep an equilibrium in marine biological systems.

6.3. Contamination and Beach front Turn of events:

Beach front contamination, including supplement overflow from horticulture and metropolitan regions, can add to jellyfish sprouts by advancing the development of phytoplankton, an essential food hotspot for jellyfish. Furthermore, natural surroundings annihilation because of waterfront improvement can influence the accessibility of reasonable substrate for polyp settlement, influencing the general life pattern of jellyfish. Relieving the effect of contamination and waterfront advancement is significant for safeguarding the fragile equilibrium of marine environments.

Future Headings in Jellyfish Exploration:

Headways in innovation and exploration techniques offer new roads for investigating the characterization, variety, and biological jobs of jellyfish species. From hereditary examinations to remote detecting innovations, continuous and future exploration tries add to a more profound comprehension of these baffling animals.

7.1. Sub-atomic Science and Hereditary qualities:

Late headways in sub-atomic science and hereditary qualities have given specialists devices to disentangle the hereditary premise of jellyfish variations and variety. Genomic concentrates on offer experiences into the transformative connections between various jellyfish species and the atomic components fundamental their exceptional elements.

7.2. Independent Submerged Vehicles (AUVs) and Remote Detecting:

Independent Submerged Vehicles (AUVs) furnished with cutting edge sensors empower researchers to investigate the sea profundities and study jellyfish conduct right at home. Remote detecting advances, including satellite symbolism, add to checking jellyfish blossoms for a bigger scope, helping with the comprehension of their dispersion and elements.

7.3. Resident Science and Public Commitment:

Connecting with the general population in jellyfish research through resident science drives considers the assortment of significant information on jellyfish sightings, conduct, and dissemination. Public mindfulness and inclusion add to a more extensive comprehension of the natural significance of jellyfish and the requirement for protection endeavors.

1.2 Habitat Preferences and Global Distribution

The World's seas, covering more than 70% of the planet's surface, have an astounding variety of marine life. From the sunlit surface waters to the secretive profundities of the void, every marine natural surroundings is portrayed by remarkable physical and compound circumstances, molding the circulation and conduct of its occupants. This thorough investigation digs into the territory inclinations and worldwide dispersion of marine life, incorporating many living beings from minute tiny fish to goliath whales.

Sea Zones and Actual Qualities:

To comprehend the living space inclinations and circulation of marine life, it is essential to perceive the particular sea zones and their actual attributes. The sea is routinely partitioned into a few zones in view of profundity, each introducing a particular arrangement of conditions that impact the kinds of creatures that can flourish there.

1.1. Epipelagic Zone:

The epipelagic zone, otherwise called the daylight or euphotic zone, stretches out starting from the surface to roughly 200 meters. This zone gets plentiful daylight, permitting photosynthesis to happen. Therefore, it is home to a different cluster of marine life, including phytoplankton, zooplankton, fish, and marine well evolved creatures.

1.2. Mesopelagic Zone:

Underneath the epipelagic zone lies the mesopelagic, or strange place, which reaches out from 200 to 1000 meters. Light entrance is restricted in this zone, and living beings have adjusted to low light circumstances. Numerous species display vertical movement, rising to the surface around evening time to take care of and plummeting during the day to keep away from hunters.

1.3. Bathypelagic Zone:

The bathypelagic zone ranges from 1000 to 4000 meters and is described by complete dimness. Variations to outrageous tension and negligible light are apparent in the organic entities occupying this zone, including remote ocean fish, cephalopods, and bioluminescent species.

1.4. Abyssopelagic Zone:

Reaching out from 4000 meters to the sea depths, the abyssopelagic zone is the domain of the deep plain. Creatures in this zone are adjusted to the high tensions and low temperatures tracked down in the profound sea. Exceptional and ineffectively figured out species, including remote ocean vent networks, occupy this secretive climate.

1.5. Hadalpelagic Zone:

The hadalpelagic zone addresses the sea's most profound locales, including channels and remote ocean vents. Life in this outrageous climate faces high tensions as well as the difficulties of adjusting to aqueous vents, where chemosynthetic microorganisms structure the premise of the food web.

Variations to Natural surroundings Conditions:

Marine life forms show a horde of variations to flourish in their particular living spaces. These variations range from physiological and conduct characteristics to specific designs that empower endurance despite assorted natural difficulties.

2.1. Temperature Resilience:

Different marine territories present shifting temperature ranges, from the warm surface waters of tropical oceans to the close frigid temperatures of polar areas. Living beings have developed explicit temperature resiliences, and an are equipped for movement to reasonable temperature ranges during various life stages.

2.2. Saltiness Transformations:

Saltiness, the grouping of disintegrated salts in seawater, changes across various sea conditions. Species dwelling in estuaries, where freshwater meets the ocean, have developed novel physiological transformations to adapt to changes in saltiness. In the mean time, marine living beings in untamed sea conditions have specific osmoregulatory components to keep up with interior salt equilibrium.

2.3. Pressure Opposition:

The strain in the sea increments with profundity, arriving at outrageous levels in the hadalpelagic zone. Remote ocean life forms have advanced transformations, for example, adaptable body structures, compressible bodies, and concentrated chemicals to flourish under high tensions.

2.4. Bioluminescence:

Bioluminescence is a captivating transformation seen in different marine life forms, especially in the mesopelagic and bathypelagic zones where regular light is scant. Bioluminescent presentations fill numerous needs, including drawing in mates, deflecting hunters, and baiting prey.

2.5. Cover and Hue:

Cover and hue are essential variations for marine organic entities to stay away from hunters or snare prey. From the energetic tints of coral reef occupants to the straightforward groups of remote ocean animals, these variations assume a key part in the step by step processes for surviving of marine life.

Coral Reefs: Biodiversity Areas of interest:

Coral reefs are among the most assorted and useful biological systems in the sea. Framed by the aggregation of coral skeletons after some time, these lively territories support an exceptional cluster of marine life. Understanding the variables affecting coral reef dissemination and biodiversity gives bits of knowledge into the sensitive equilibrium that supports these remarkable environments.

3.1. Coral Advantageous interaction:

Corals structure harmonious associations with photosynthetic green growth called zooxanthellae. This beneficial interaction is a main impetus behind the progress of coral reefs, as the green growth give the corals supplements through photosynthesis. Coral reefs flourish in shallow, sunlit waters where this advantageous relationship can thrive.

3.2. Dangers to Coral Reefs:

Coral reefs face various dangers, including increasing ocean temperatures, sea fermentation, contamination, and overfishing. Coral blanching, a peculiarity where corals remove their harmonious green growth, is an outcome of stressors like expanded temperatures. Understanding and alleviating these dangers are significant for the protection of coral reef environments.

Worldwide Conveyance of Marine Life:

The conveyance of marine life is impacted by a horde of variables, including actual oceanography, supplement accessibility, and the collaborations between species. Inspecting the worldwide circulation designs gives significant experiences into the interconnectedness of marine biological systems on a planetary scale.

4.1. Sea Flows and Gyres:

Sea flows assume a urgent part in the conveyance of marine living beings, impacting the dispersal of hatchlings, the vehicle of supplements, and the development of transient species. Huge scope gyres, like the North Atlantic Gyre and the South Pacific Gyre, have particular natural attributes that shape the conveyance of marine life inside them.

4.2. Upwelling Zones:

Upwelling zones, where supplement rich profound waters ascend to the surface, make exceptionally useful regions that help different marine environments. These locales are described by expanded phytoplankton overflow, drawing in an outpouring of marine life, from zooplankton to huge pelagic hunters.

4.3. Relocation and Occasional Examples:

Numerous marine species display transitory way of behaving, getting across tremendous distances in light of changing ecological circumstances or life cycle prerequisites. Occasional examples, impacted by elements like temperature and food accessibility, add to the unique dissemination of marine life in various locales over time.

4.4. Seaside Biological systems:

Seaside biological systems, including estuaries, mangroves, and salt bogs, are essential environments that act as nurseries for various marine species. These regions are described by an intricate interchange of freshwater and marine impacts, giving a rich and different climate for both inhabitant and transitory species.

Human Effect on Marine Circulation:

Human exercises, going from overfishing to contamination and environmental change, significantly affect the circulation of marine life. Understanding the anthropogenic variables affecting marine biological systems is fundamental for creating practical preservation and the board techniques.

5.1. Overfishing and Consumption of Assets:

Overfishing, driven by expanded interest for fish, has prompted the consumption of fish stocks and modified the elements of marine food networks. The breakdown of specific fisheries has flowing consequences for the circulation and overflow of species all through the environment.

5.2. Contamination and Living space Corruption:

Contamination, including plastic garbage, oil slicks, and supplement overflow, represents a huge danger to marine natural surroundings. Beach front regions, specifically, are defenseless against environment corruption because of urbanization and modern exercises, influencing the appropriation of species that depend on these biological systems.

5.3. Environmental Change and Sea Warming:

Environmental change, driven by anthropogenic exercises, adds to climbing ocean temperatures, sea fermentation, and changes in precipitation designs. These adjustments have broad ramifications for marine life, influencing the circulation of species, the planning of conceptive occasions, and the design of environments.

Protection and Supportable Administration:

Safeguarding the variety and dispersion of marine life requires purposeful endeavors in protection and practical administration. Carrying out methodologies to alleviate anthropogenic effects and safeguard basic territories is fundamental for defending the wellbeing and flexibility of marine biological systems.

6.1. Marine Safeguarded Regions (MPAs):

Marine Safeguarded Regions assume a vital part in saving biodiversity and supporting the recuperation of drained species. By assigning explicit zones where human exercises are confined, MPAs add to the protection of fundamental natural surroundings and the support of solid marine populaces.

6.2. Feasible Fisheries The executives:

Embracing economical fisheries the board rehearses is fundamental for forestalling overfishing and advancing the drawn out strength of marine environments. Measures, for example, size limits, get quantities, and the execution of stuff guidelines add to keeping up with the harmony between human double-dealing and the strength of fish populaces.

6.3. Environmental Change Alleviation and Transformation:

Tending to the effects of environmental change on marine life requires worldwide endeavors to alleviate ozone harming substance emanations and adjust to changing ecological circumstances. Examination into versatile species and environments, as well as the improvement of imaginative preservation procedures, is pivotal for exploring the difficulties presented by a quickly evolving environment.

Future Points of view and Difficulties:

As humankind keeps on investigating, exploit, and change the seas, the eventual fate of marine life is complicatedly connected to our capacity to address arising difficulties and embrace economical practices. Continuous examination, innovative progressions, and worldwide cooperation are fundamental for exploring the intricacies of marine environment inclinations and worldwide appropriation.

7.1. Mechanical Progressions in Marine Exploration:

The improvement of cutting edge innovations, including independent submerged vehicles (AUVs), remotely worked vehicles (ROVs), and satellite-based observing frameworks, has altered our capacity to concentrate on marine life and biological systems. These apparatuses give remarkable admittance to remote ocean conditions, empowering scientists to archive and grasp the circulation of species in beforehand blocked off regions.

7.2. Incorporated Ways to deal with Preservation:

The preservation of marine environments and biodiversity requires incorporated approaches that think about the interconnectedness of biological systems and the total effects of human exercises. Cooperative endeavors among researchers, policymakers, and nearby networks are fundamental for creating powerful protection techniques that address numerous stressors at the same time.

7.3. Public Mindfulness and Training:

Raising public mindfulness about the significance of marine environments and the dangers they face is critical for cultivating a feeling of obligation and empowering reasonable practices. Schooling and effort drives add to informed independent direction and enable people to settle on decisions that help the soundness of the seas.

1.3 Anatomy and Physiology of Jellyfish

Jellyfish, with their elegant, undulating developments and hypnotizing clear bodies, possess a novel spot in the huge domain of marine life. To genuinely see the value in these cryptic animals, it is fundamental to dig into the complexities of their life structures and physiology. From the specific designs that characterize their bodies to the physiological cycles that empower their endurance, this far reaching investigation expects to disclose the interesting universe of jellyfish at the cell, tissue, and organismal levels.

Fundamental Life structures of Jellyfish:

Jellyfish, experimentally named Cnidarians, display a straightforward yet exquisite body plan portrayed by a coagulated umbrella-formed chime and following limbs. Understanding the key physical elements is crucial to disentangling the secrets of their science.

1.1. Ringer Construction:

The ringer, or medusa, is the unmistakable, umbrella-formed part of the jellyfish. Made basically out of a coagulated substance called mesoglea, the chime offers primary help and lightness. The ringer's shape and size shift among species, adding to the unmistakable appearance of changed jellyfish.

1.2. Appendages and Nematocysts:

Following from the edge of the ringer are appendages furnished with particular stinging cells known as nematocysts. Nematocysts are tiny, spear like designs containing toxin. These cells are utilized for prey catch, protection against hunters, and, surprisingly, in specific species for movement. The variety of nematocysts adds to the variety of cautious and savage procedures utilized by various jellyfish species.

1.3. Oral Arms and Mouth:

Underneath the chime, some jellyfish have oral arms that stretch out descending, encompassing the mouth. The mouth fills in as both an entry and exit for food and waste. While not all jellyfish have clear cut oral arms, their presence is remarkable in specific species, like the lion's mane jellyfish (Cyanea capillata).

1.4. Gastrovascular Cavity:

Jellyfish need complex organ frameworks however have a gastrovascular pit that serves different capabilities. This cavity goes about as both a stomach related chamber and a circulatory framework. In the wake of catching prey with their arms, jellyfish utilize the mouth to move the food into the gastrovascular cavity, where absorption happens. Supplements are then disseminated all through the jellyfish's body by means of dispersion.

Cell Level: Cells and Tissues:

At the cell level, jellyfish show surprising effortlessness yet complexity. The association of cells and tissues adds to the fundamental capabilities essential for their endurance.

2.1. Epidermis and Gastrodermis:

The external layer of the jellyfish, known as the epidermis, gives security and fills in as a boundary against outside components. Underneath the epidermis lies the gastrodermis, which lines the internal surface of the ringer and appendages. The gastrodermis contains particular cells liable for assimilation and supplement retention.

2.2. Mesoglea:

The mesoglea, the coagulated substance between the epidermis and gastrodermis, adds to the jellyfish's lightness and underlying trustworthiness. Made essentially out of water, collagen, and different proteins, the mesoglea's properties fluctuate among species and can influence the jellyfish's general structure and development.

2.3. Nerve Net:

Jellyfish come up short on incorporated sensory system, like a mind, yet have a decentralized organization of interconnected nerve cells called a nerve net. This nerve net takes into account simple tactile insight and coordination of developments. The effortlessness of the nerve net adds to the decentralized control saw in jellyfish ways of behaving.

Physiological Cycles:

The physiology of jellyfish incorporates a scope of cycles that empower them to explore their current circumstance, catch prey, and answer different improvements. From headway to proliferation, understanding these physiological components reveals insight into the versatile systems created by jellyfish north of millions of years.

3.1. Motion:

Jellyfish display a novel method of velocity described by throbs of the chime. Constrictions of the ringer remove water, moving the jellyfish forward. The effortlessness of this swimming component misrepresents its viability, permitting jellyfish to move with amazing beauty and productivity. Certain species can likewise display fly impetus by strongly ousting water from the chime, empowering quick developments.

3.2. Taking care of and Assimilation:

Jellyfish are meat eating and fundamentally feed on little fish, tiny fish, and other coagulated creatures. Utilizing their following arms outfitted with nematocysts, jellyfish catch prey. Upon contact, nematocysts discharge toxin, immobilizing the prey, which is then moved to the mouth for ingestion. The gastrovascular cavity works with extracellular assimilation, separating the prey into supplements that diffuse into the jellyfish's cells.

3.3. Propagation:

Jellyfish utilize both sexual and abiogenetic generation in their life cycles. Abiogenetic proliferation includes the arrangement of polyps, which bud off adolescent jellyfish known as ephyrae. Sexual propagation includes the arrival of eggs and sperm into the water, prompting the improvement of planula hatchlings. These hatchlings in the end choose a substrate, shaping polyps and finishing the existence cycle. The capacity of specific jellyfish species, for example, Turritopsis dohrnii, to return to a prior life stage has accumulated consideration for its possible ramifications in everlasting status.

3.4. Ecological Detecting:

While lacking modern tangible organs, jellyfish have essential instruments for natural detecting. The nerve net considers the view of changes in the environmental elements, empowering jellyfish to answer boosts like light, temperature, and flows. A few animal types show diel vertical relocation, climbing to surface waters around evening time and slipping during the day, possibly because of changes in light levels.

Particular Transformations and One of a kind Ways of behaving:

Jellyfish have developed a horde of particular variations and extraordinary ways of behaving that add to their endurance in different marine conditions. These transformations range from the capacity to endure changing temperatures to the hypnotizing bioluminescence showed by specific species.

4.1. Temperature Resilience:

Jellyfish possess many maritime conditions, from polar districts to tropical oceans. A few animal types show surprising temperature resistance, adjusting to the particular warm states of their natural surroundings. This versatility adds to the worldwide circulation of jellyfish and their capacity to flourish in shifted environments.

4.2. Bioluminescence:

Bioluminescence is a striking variation showed by specific jellyfish species. This peculiarity includes the development of light through a synthetic response inside particular cells called photocytes. Bioluminescence fills numerous needs, including drawing in mates, discouraging hunters, and tricking prey in the murkiness of the remote ocean.

4.3. Chime Shape and Throbs:

The particular ringer state of jellyfish and their throbbing developments are fundamental parts of their step by step process for surviving. The chime's shape influences the proficiency of swimming and lightness, while throbs control the jellyfish's drive through the water. The straightforwardness of this velocity component adds to the energy effectiveness of jellyfish swimming.

4.4. Polymorphism and Life Cycle Variations:

Jellyfish display polymorphism, wherein people of similar species can take on various structures during different phases of their life cycle. This flexibility permits jellyfish to take advantage of various natural specialties. Life cycle transformations, for example, the capacity to switch among polyp and medusa stages, add to their biological achievement and versatility in unique marine conditions.

Jellyfish Cooperations with the Climate:

The cooperations among jellyfish and their current circumstance are multi-layered, impacting natural elements, supplement cycling, and the more extensive marine biological system. From their jobs as hunters and prey to their reactions to ecological changes, jellyfish assume essential parts in keeping up with the fragile equilibrium of marine biological systems.

5.1. Trophic Associations:

Jellyfish take part in trophic communications as the two hunters and prey. Their predation on planktonic organic entities and little fish influences the overflow and piece of prey populaces. All the while, jellyfish act as a food hotspot for different marine hunters, including ocean turtles, certain fish species, and seabirds.

5.2. Impact on Fish Populaces:

Jellyfish sprouts, portrayed by the quick expansion in jellyfish overflow, can affect fish populaces by outcompeting them for assets or straightforwardly originating before on fish eggs and hatchlings. The outcomes of jellyfish-fish cooperations shift and rely upon variables like natural circumstances, prey accessibility, and the particular species included.

5.3. Supplement Cycling:

Jellyfish add to supplement burnning in marine environments through their taking care of and discharge processes. By catching and processing prey, jellyfish discharge supplements once more into the water, impacting supplement accessibility and cycling. This job in supplement elements has suggestions for essential efficiency and the general wellbeing of marine environments.

Jellyfish Blossoms: Causes and Outcomes:

Jellyfish blossoms, characterized by the fast expansion of jellyfish populaces, stand out because of their natural ramifications and possible connects to human exercises. Understanding the causes and results of jellyfish blossoms is essential for dealing with their effect on marine environments.

6.1. Ecological Triggers:

Jellyfish sprouts can be set off by a mix of ecological variables, including water temperature, supplement accessibility, and changes in sea flows. Certain human-actuated changes, for example, overfishing, eutrophication, and environmental change, can make conditions helpful for jellyfish multiplication.

6.2. Natural Results:

The natural results of jellyfish blossoms are different and influence different parts of marine biological systems. Contest with fish for food assets, predation on fish eggs and hatchlings, and change of supplement cycling are among the impacts that can impact the construction and elements of marine food networks.

6.3. Human Communications and Difficulties:

Jellyfish blossoms present difficulties for human exercises, including fisheries, the travel industry, and beach front turn of events. Blossoms can prompt the consumption of fish stocks, obstruct fishing stuff, and effect hydroponics activities. Creating methodologies to relieve the effect of jellyfish blossoms on human exercises requires a nuanced comprehension of the biological elements included.

Protection and The board:

The protection and supportable administration of jellyfish populaces include tending to both normal and anthropogenic variables that impact their overflow and dispersion. Protection endeavors intend to safeguard the natural jobs of jellyfish while alleviating possible adverse consequences on human exercises.

7.1. Grasping Natural Jobs:

Perceiving the environmental jobs of jellyfish in marine biological systems is basic to their protection. As opposed to survey jellyfish exclusively as disturbances or contenders, grasping their commitments to supplement cycling, trophic cooperations, and generally environment wellbeing illuminates more all encompassing protection draws near.

7.2. Manageable Fisheries Practices:

Carrying out economical fisheries rehearses is vital for overseeing cooperations among jellyfish and monetarily significant fish stocks. Measures, for example, biological system based fisheries the executives, gear changes, and mindful reaping add to keeping a harmony among jellyfish and fish populaces.

7.3. Checking and Early Admonition Frameworks:

Checking jellyfish populaces and ecological circumstances is fundamental for anticipating and answering jellyfish blossoms. Early admonition frameworks can give significant data to fisheries, hydroponics tasks, and beach front networks, considering versatile administration techniques in light of changing jellyfish elements.

Future Viewpoints in Jellyfish Exploration:

The field of jellyfish research keeps on developing, driven by innovative headways, interdisciplinary coordinated efforts, and the developing acknowledgment of the biological significance of these living beings. Future examination attempts hold the commitment of unwinding extra secrets encompassing jellyfish science and their connections with marine environments.

8.1. Genomic and Sub-atomic Investigations:

Progressions in genomic and sub-atomic examinations offer chances to investigate the hereditary premise of jellyfish transformations, life cycle advances, and their reactions to ecological changes. Opening the atomic components hidden jellyfish physiology gives bits of knowledge into their developmental history and potential for variation.

8.2. Effect of Environmental Change:

Environmental change presents difficulties for marine biological systems, and understanding how jellyfish answer climbing ocean temperatures, sea fermentation, and other environment related stressors is a key exploration center. Exploring the expected changes in jellyfish dissemination and overflow under various environment situations illuminates protection and the board methodologies.

8.3. Resident Science and Public Commitment:

Connecting with general society in jellyfish research through resident science drives encourages a more extensive comprehension of marine biology and preservation. Public support in checking jellyfish sightings, adding to explore endeavors, and advancing mindful beach front practices improves mindfulness and engages networks to effectively take part in saving marine biological systems.

Chapter 2

Feeding And Predatory Tactics

Jellyfish, with their ethereal appearance and enthralling developments, are entrancing in their science as well as charming in their taking care of systems and ruthless strategies. In spite of their apparently fragile nature, jellyfish are productive and deft hunters that have developed a scope of strategies to catch and consume their prey. This investigation digs into the complexities of jellyfish taking care of, from the particular designs engaged with prey catch to the natural jobs they play as the two hunters and prey in marine biological systems.

Taking care of Designs and Concentrated Transformations:

The taking care of components of jellyfish are a demonstration of the tastefulness of development, displaying particular designs that permit these organic entities to take advantage of an assortment of prey in their maritime surroundings.

1.1. Appendages and Nematocysts:

The essential taking care of mechanical assembly of jellyfish is their following appendages, which reach out from the ringer. These limbs are furnished with particular stinging cells called nematocysts. Nematocysts are minute cases containing a curled, spear like string and toxin. When set off by contact with prey, the nematocysts quickly release, infusing toxin and immobilizing the objective.

The variety of nematocysts among jellyfish species adds to the flexibility of their ruthless strategies. Some nematocysts entrap and trap prey, while others enter the prey's body, conveying poisons that deaden or kill. This variety of nematocysts permits jellyfish to catch an extensive variety of prey, from little scavangers and fish hatchlings to other coagulated life forms.

1.2. Oral Arms and Mouth:

Underneath the chime, certain jellyfish species have oral arms that encompass the mouth. These designs are engaged with the vehicle of caught prey to the focal mouth for ingestion. While not all jellyfish have clear cut oral arms, their presence is prominent in species like the lion's mane jellyfish (Cyanea capillata). The oral arms, with expansions of the gastrovascular pit, help in the control and handling of food.

1.3. Gastrovascular Pit:

The gastrovascular hole is a focal element in jellyfish life structures that serves both as a stomach related chamber and a circulatory framework. Whenever prey is caught by the arms, it is moved to the mouth and into the gastrovascular pit. Inside this depression, extracellular assimilation happens, worked with by proteins emitted by gastrodermal cells. The subsequent supplements are then disseminated all through the jellyfish's body by means of dispersion.

The effortlessness of the gastrovascular pit features the proficiency with which jellyfish separate supplements from their prey. While lacking particular stomach related organs, jellyfish have adjusted to flourish in their surroundings by using a decentralized and powerful framework for supplement retention.

Savage Strategies and Systems:

Jellyfish display different ruthless strategies and methodologies that add to their prosperity as pioneering feeders in marine biological systems. These strategies are formed by variables, for example, the kind of prey accessible, the climate they possess, and the transformative variations intended for every jellyfish species.

2.1. Snare Predation:

Some jellyfish species utilize snare predation, ready to pounce for clueless prey to come into contact with their arms. The nematocysts on the limbs are set off by the dash of prey, starting a fast reaction to catch and immobilize the objective. This strategy is especially compelling in catching little fish, microscopic fish, and other coagulated organic entities that float into the jellyfish's area.

Trap hunters frequently have appendages decorated with nematocysts of fluctuating sizes and works. This variety permits them to catch an expansive range of prey, adjusting to the particular difficulties introduced by various life forms in their current circumstance.

2.2. Dynamic Hunting:

While some jellyfish are trap hunters, others participate in dynamic hunting ways of behaving. These jellyfish effectively swim and seek after their prey, utilizing both their arms and ringer for successful catch. Dynamic trackers might display complex swimming examples, utilizing their ringer throbs to move them forward while stretching out and withdrawing their arms to catch prey reachable.

The capacity to effectively chase gives specific jellyfish species a benefit in conditions where prey is scattered or while experiencing more portable creatures. This methodology permits them to cover bigger regions and effectively search out potential food sources.

2.3. Prey Entrapment and Immobilization:

Jellyfish use their appendages for catching prey as well as for trapping and immobilizing it successfully. The nematocysts on the limbs assume a vital part in this cycle. Upon contact with prey, the nematocysts discharge poisons that deaden or debilitate the objective, forestalling escape.

The cement properties of some nematocysts empower jellyfish to trap and get their prey, making a web-like design that thwarts the development of caught life forms. This system is especially powerful while managing more modest or more sensitive prey that might endeavor to escape.

Environmental Jobs as Hunters and Prey:

Jellyfish assume fundamental parts in marine biological systems as the two hunters and prey, adding to the equilibrium and elements of food networks. Their associations with different creatures, including bigger hunters and their own conspecifics, shape the design and working of the marine climate.

3.1. Trophic Associations:

Jellyfish take part in trophic collaborations by possessing different situations in marine food networks. As hunters, they apply strain on populaces of tiny fish, little fish, and other coagulated living beings. All the while, jellyfish act as a food hotspot for higher trophic levels, including bigger fish, ocean turtles, and certain seabirds.

The unique trophic communications including jellyfish impact the overflow and conveyance of prey species, possibly influencing the sythesis of whole biological systems. Understanding these communications is urgent for anticipating the flowing impacts of jellyfish on marine food networks.

3.2. Rivalry with Fish:

Jellyfish frequently contend with fish for comparable prey assets, particularly in conditions where the two gatherings are bountiful. The crafty taking care of techniques of jellyfish, joined with their capacity to take advantage of a different scope of prey, can prompt rivalry with fish for food assets. Now and again, jellyfish may outcompete fish for planktonic living beings, affecting the construction of the neighborhood fish local area.

3.3. Predation on Fish Eggs and Hatchlings:

Certain jellyfish species assume a part in molding fish populaces by going after their eggs and hatchlings. The appendages of jellyfish, outfitted with nematocysts, can catch fish eggs and hatchlings as they float in the water segment. This predation can impact the enlistment progress of fish populaces and add to the normal guideline of fish overflow in marine biological systems.

Ecological Elements Affecting Taking care of Conduct:

Jellyfish taking care of conduct is impacted by different ecological variables, including temperature, supplement accessibility, and the presence of reasonable prey. These variables add to the powerful idea of jellyfish populaces and their cooperations with different living beings in the marine climate.

4.1. Temperature:

Temperature assumes a vital part in forming the taking care of conduct of jellyfish. Various species have temperature inclinations that impact their metabolic rates and generally speaking action levels. Hotter temperatures might upgrade the metabolic cycles engaged with processing and supplement ingestion, possibly impacting taking care of rates and the outcome of jellyfish populaces.

4.2. Supplement Accessibility:

The accessibility of supplements in the water section is a key variable impacting the dissemination and overflow of prey organic entities, which, thus, influences jellyfish taking care of. Supplement rich conditions, for example, upwelling zones and regions with high essential efficiency, give more than adequate food assets to jellyfish. Changes in supplement accessibility, whether normal or anthropogenic, can affect the outcome of jellyfish populaces.

4.3. Prey Overflow and Piece:

The overflow and piece of prey creatures in the general climate fundamentally impact jellyfish taking care of conduct. Jellyfish are astute feeders, changing their strategies in light of the accessibility and kind of prey. Blossoms of microscopic fish or other thick life forms can set off expanded taking care of movement, prompting the fast multiplication of jellyfish populaces during specific ecological circumstances.

Human Effect on Jellyfish Taking care of:

Human exercises, going from overfishing to contamination and environmental change, significantly affect the taking care of conduct of jellyfish. Understanding the anthropogenic variables affecting jellyfish populaces is fundamental for dealing with their effect on marine biological systems and moderating likely contentions with human exercises.

5.1. Overfishing and Trophic Fountains:

Overfishing, especially of monetarily significant fish species, can prompt uneven characters in marine food networks and impact the elements of jellyfish populaces. Decreased predation strain on jellyfish prey, combined with the expulsion of contending fish species, may add to the multiplication of jellyfish populaces. This peculiarity, known as a trophic fountain, highlights the interconnected idea of marine environments and the results of modifying hunter prey elements.

5.2. Eutrophication and Modified Supplement Elements:

Eutrophication, the extreme contribution of supplements into oceanic biological systems, can prompt changes in supplement elements that favor jellyfish. Raised supplement levels can invigorate the development of planktonic living beings, giving a plentiful food source to jellyfish. Also, eutrophication can add to the development of no man's lands, regions with low oxygen levels, which may specifically help jellyfish species adjusted to low-oxygen conditions.

5.3. Environmental Change and Sea Warming:

Environmental change, driven by human exercises, adds to climbing ocean temperatures and adjustments in maritime circumstances. These progressions can impact the circulation and conduct of jellyfish, affecting their taking care of examples and cooperations with other marine life forms. Changes in the timing and force of jellyfish blossoms have been connected to environment related factors, featuring the need to think about the more extensive biological outcomes of worldwide ecological changes.

Alleviation and The board Methodologies:

Dealing with the effect of jellyfish on marine environments and human exercises requires the advancement of relief and the board methodologies. These procedures intend to address both normal and anthropogenic variables affecting jellyfish populaces while advancing the maintainability of marine conditions.

6.1. Feasible Fisheries The board:

Executing supportable fisheries the board rehearses is urgent for keeping up with the harmony among jellyfish and financially important fish stocks. Environment based fisheries the executives, which considers the more extensive biological setting, forestalls overfishing and limit the potential for trophic fountains that favor jellyfish.

6.2. Checking and Early Admonition Frameworks:

Checking jellyfish populaces and ecological circumstances is fundamental for anticipating and answering potential issues connected with their taking care of conduct. Early admonition frameworks, upheld by trend setting innovations and information assortment, can give important data to fisheries, hydroponics activities, and beach front networks. This empowers ideal and versatile administration methodologies to relieve the effect of jellyfish sprouts.

6.3. Coordinated Waterfront Zone The executives:

Coordinated Waterfront Zone The executives (ICZM) approaches think about the intricate connections among jellyfish and their current circumstance inside a more extensive beach front administration structure. ICZM includes composed endeavors to address various stressors, including contamination, living space corruption, and overfishing, which can impact jellyfish populaces. By taking on an all encompassing point of view, ICZM advances the feasible utilization of beach front assets and the conservation of environment wellbeing.

2.1 Feeding Mechanisms: Stinging Cells and Tentacles

Jellyfish, with their elegant developments and clear bodies, utilize shrewd taking care of systems that make them productive hunters in the marine climate. At the core of their ruthless achievement are particular designs known as stinging cells (nematocysts) and limbs. This investigation digs into the perplexing universe of jellyfish taking care of, unwinding the components that permit them to catch and consume a different scope of prey.

Stinging Cells (Nematocysts):

The foundation of jellyfish taking care of lies in their amazing stinging cells, logically alluded to as nematocysts. These minuscule, spear like designs are dispersed along the outer layer of the jellyfish's arms and different limbs. Nematocysts are a characterizing component of the phylum Cnidaria, to which jellyfish have a place, and their complexity is vital to the savage outcome of jellyfish.

1.1. Design of Nematocysts:

Nematocysts comprise of a case containing a firmly wound, string like design called a cnidocil. Encompassing the container is a defensive layer that keeps the nematocyst in a torpid state until set off. When a nematocyst is enacted, the cnidocil faculties mechanical or substance improvements, prompting a fast ejection of the wound string.

The catapulted string, looking like a smaller than usual spear, enters the objective living being, infusing toxin and frequently immobilizing the prey. The variety of nematocyst types among jellyfish species adds to the adaptability of their savage methodologies. Some nematocysts are intended for trapping and catching prey, while others are particular for infusing toxin straightforwardly into the prey.

1.2. Flexibility of Nematocysts:

Jellyfish display an astounding variety of nematocyst types, each adjusted to explicit capabilities in the ruthless cycle. Coming up next are a few normal sorts of nematocysts tracked down in jellyfish:

Stenotele: These nematocysts are little and add to the cement properties of the limbs, helping with the snare of prey.

Desmoneme: Tracked down in specific species, desmonemes are portrayed by lengthy, slim strings that are productive in catching little prey.

Spirocyst: Spirocysts have an extraordinary winding molded string, and they are many times engaged with immobilizing bigger prey.

Atrichous Isorhiza: Atrichous isorhizas need spikes on their strings and are associated with envenomating prey without essentially catching them.

Birhopaloid: This kind of nematocyst has two long strings, giving a compelling method for snaring and quelling prey.

The mix of these nematocyst types permits jellyfish to adjust their ruthless procedures to various prey sizes, types, and natural circumstances.

Limbs: Augmentations of Savage Greatness

Limbs are the outside extremities of jellyfish that house the nematocysts and assume a focal part in their taking care of components. These adaptable and frequently stretched structures reach out from the edge of the ringer, framing a perplexing organization intended for prey catch, control, and transport.

2.1. Construction and Arrangement:

Jellyfish arms are made out of layers of specific cells, including epidermal and gastrodermal cells. The external layer, or epidermis, gives security and houses the nematocysts. The internal layer, or gastrodermis, is associated with the vehicle of caught prey to the focal mouth for processing.

Appendages shift long and thickness among jellyfish species, reflecting variations to their environmental specialties and prey inclinations. A few animal types have long, following limbs intended for catching prey a ways off, while others have more limited appendages appropriate for tight situation experiences.

2.2. Prey Catch and Immobilization:

Appendages act as the essential means by which jellyfish catch their prey. The nematocysts, implanted in the epidermal cells of the arms, are decisively situated to amplify contact with expected prey. At the point when a jellyfish experiences a reasonable objective, the nematocysts on the limbs are set off, sending off a fast reaction to catch and immobilize the prey.

The productivity of this cycle lies in the coordination between the nematocysts, the limbs, and the general way of behaving of the jellyfish. A few animal groups show complex swimming examples to effectively search out prey, while others depend on latent floating and snare strategies to catch living beings that come into contact with their limbs.

Taking care of Cycle: From Catch to Absorption

The taking care of cycle of jellyfish includes a succession of occasions from prey catch to processing inside the gastrovascular pit. Understanding this cycle gives bits of knowledge into the proficiency and versatility of jellyfish as hunters in different marine conditions.

3.1. Prey Catch:

The underlying move toward the taking care of interaction is the catch of prey utilizing the specific nematocysts on the appendages. As the nematocysts are set off upon contact, they release their spear like strings, infusing toxin into the prey. This toxin serves to immobilize or stifle the objective, keeping it from getting away from the grasp of the appendages.

The flexibility of nematocysts permits jellyfish to catch an extensive variety of prey, from minuscule tiny fish to little fish. The ensnaring and immobilizing properties of certain nematocysts add to the adequacy of the catch cycle.

3.2. Transport to the Mouth:

When the prey is caught, the limbs assume a critical part in shipping it to the focal mouth situated at the underside of the jellyfish's ringer. The limbs move the caught prey through the water, limiting the energy consumption expected for prey transport.

Species with oral arms, like the lion's mane jellyfish, may likewise utilize these designs to support the control and transport of prey towards the mouth. The oral arms encompass the mouth and can assist with directing caught creatures into the gastrovascular depression for processing.

3.3. Processing in the Gastrovascular Cavity:

Jellyfish miss the mark on obvious stomach or complex stomach related organs, however they have a gastrovascular hole where processing happens. The gastrodermal cells coating the pit discharge proteins that separate the caught prey into more straightforward mixtures, working with supplement retention.

The course of extracellular assimilation inside the gastrovascular hole is an illustration of the decentralized idea of jellyfish physiology. Supplements got from the processed prey are then appropriated all through the jellyfish's body by means of dissemination, supporting its energy needs and supporting its by and large organic capabilities.

Job of Taking care of Components in Nature:

The taking care of components of jellyfish assume essential parts in marine nature, impacting the elements of food networks, supplement cycling, and the cooperations among jellyfish and other marine life forms.

4.1. Trophic Communications:

Jellyfish take part in trophic connections as the two hunters and prey. Their job in marine food networks includes impacting the overflow and dispersion of planktonic organic entities, little fish, and other thick life forms. While filling in as hunters to these gatherings, jellyfish likewise give a critical food source to higher trophic levels, including bigger fish, ocean turtles, and certain seabirds.

The harmony between jellyfish predation and their commitment to higher trophic levels is fundamental for keeping up with the general wellbeing and solidness of marine biological systems. Understanding these trophic connections is vital to anticipating the flowing impacts of jellyfish on different parts of the food web.

4.2. Supplement Cycling:

Jellyfish add to supplement burnning in marine environments through their taking care of and assimilation processes. As they catch and condensation prey, supplements are delivered once more into the water through discharge and decay. This supplement reusing has suggestions for essential efficiency and the general supplement elements of the marine climate.

Jellyfish sprouts, portrayed by the quick expansion in jellyfish overflow, can improve supplement cycling, possibly impacting the accessibility of supplements for other marine organic entities. The environmental outcomes of jellyfish-interceded supplement cycling highlight their diverse jobs in marine biological systems.

Ecological Elements Affecting Taking care of Conduct:

The taking care of conduct of jellyfish is impacted by a horde of ecological variables that shape their dispersion, overflow, and generally accomplishment as hunters.

5.1. Temperature:

Temperature is a basic element impacting the metabolic rates and action levels of jellyfish. Various types of jellyfish have fluctuating temperature inclinations, and changes in ocean temperature can affect their taking care of conduct. Hotter temperatures might improve the proficiency of metabolic cycles engaged with assimilation and supplement ingestion, impacting the general taking care of paces of jellyfish populaces.

5.2. Saltiness:

Saltiness, the grouping of broken down salts in seawater, is another natural component influencing jellyfish physiology. Certain jellyfish species have variations to explicit saltiness ranges, and changes in saltiness can impact their dispersion and taking care of conduct. Understanding saltiness inclinations is fundamental for anticipating how jellyfish populaces might answer adjustments in waterfront conditions.

5.3. Prey Accessibility:

The overflow and piece of prey creatures in the water section straightforwardly influence jellyfish taking care of conduct. Changes in prey accessibility, whether because of normal variances or human-prompted factors, can impact the outcome of jellyfish populaces. Expanded prey accessibility can prompt upgraded taking care of rates and potential populace sprouts, while decreased prey overflow might restrict their development and proliferation.

Protection Suggestions and The executives Methodologies:

The taking care of systems of jellyfish, while essential to their environmental jobs, can present difficulties with regards to human exercises and biological system protection. Perceiving the significance of jellyfish in marine environments, and executing procedures to moderate possible struggles, is urgent for reasonable concurrence.

6.1. Feasible Fisheries The executives:

In locales where jellyfish populaces communicate with monetarily important fish stocks, maintainable fisheries the board rehearses are fundamental. Carrying out biological system based fisheries the executives thinks about the more extensive setting of trophic collaborations, planning to forestall overfishing and keep up with the harmony among jellyfish and fish populaces. By embracing an all encompassing methodology, fisheries can add to the versatility of marine environments and lessen the gamble of trophic fountains.

6.2. Observing and Early Admonition Frameworks:

Observing jellyfish populaces and ecological circumstances is fundamental for anticipating and answering potential issues connected with their taking care of conduct. Early admonition frameworks, upheld by headways in innovation and information assortment, can give significant data to fisheries, hydroponics activities, and waterfront networks. This empowers ideal and versatile administration systems to relieve the effect of jellyfish blossoms on human exercises and marine environments.

6.3. Public Mindfulness and Schooling:

Advancing public mindfulness and schooling with respect to jellyfish nature is crucial for cultivating capable waterfront rehearses. Grasping the biological significance of jellyfish, their normal ways of behaving, and the variables impacting their populaces supports a reasonable viewpoint. Drawing in seaside networks in preservation endeavors and giving data on mindful the travel industry practices can add to the conjunction of people and jellyfish in shared beach front conditions.

2.2Prey Preferences and Hunting Strategies

Jellyfish, with their ethereal appearance and apparently sensitive nature, harbor an interesting universe of savage ability underneath the outer layer of the seas. Their prey inclinations and hunting systems are multifaceted variations sharpened through advancement, empowering these thick life forms to flourish in assorted marine conditions. This investigation digs into the conundrum of jellyfish prey inclinations and the complex methodologies they utilize to catch and consume different living beings.

Prey Inclinations Across Species:

One of the noteworthy parts of jellyfish nature is their flexibility in prey choice. Various types of jellyfish display unmistakable prey inclinations, mirroring their transformative history, natural specialty, and biological job inside unambiguous marine environments.

1.1. Planktonic Living beings:

A huge part of jellyfish counts calories involves planktonic life forms, including minuscule shellfish, larval fish, and different little spineless creatures. The taking care of device of jellyfish, especially their appendages outfitted with stinging cells (nematocysts), is appropriate for catching these floating, minute prey. A few animal groups have practical experience in taking advantage of occasional sprouts of explicit planktonic organic entities, exhibiting a degree of environmental specialization in their prey inclinations.

1.2. Little Endlessly fish Hatchlings:

Certain jellyfish species have advanced to go after little endlessly fish hatchlings. Their hunting systems include effectively seeking after schools of fish or ambushing them by floating in the water flows. The nematocysts on their limbs assume a urgent part in immobilizing the fish, permitting the jellyfish to quell and consume their prey. This variation is especially huge in environments where jellyfish and fish share comparable trophic levels.

1.3. Other Thick Organic entities:

Notwithstanding planktonic living beings and little fish, jellyfish may likewise go after other thick life forms, for example, brush jams and different types of jellyfish. This intraguild predation features the mind boggling snare of associations inside marine biological systems, where jellyfish contend and coincide with other coagulated species for assets. The capacity to catch and consume other coagulated organic entities further underlines the adaptability of jellyfish taking care of techniques.

Hunting Systems:

Jellyfish utilize a different exhibit of hunting procedures to catch their favored prey. These procedures, formed by the species' morphology, conduct, and natural setting, add to the general progress of jellyfish as hunters in the marine climate.

2.1. Trap Predation:

Trap predation is a typical methodology among jellyfish, especially those that depend on floating or throbbing developments. Situated with their arms broadened, these jellyfish trust that clueless prey will come into contact with their stinging cells. The nematocysts on the limbs are set off upon contact, empowering the fast immobilization and catch of the prey. This procedure is powerful for catching planktonic living beings, little spineless creatures, and larval fish.

2.2. Dynamic Hunting:

Some jellyfish species are dynamic trackers, displaying ways of behaving, for example, swimming and pursuit to search out and catch prey effectively. Dynamic trackers utilize their ringer throbs to push themselves through the water, stretching out and withdrawing their limbs to cover a bigger region. This system is profitable in conditions where prey is scattered or while experiencing more portable organic entities. The flexibility of dynamic hunting permits jellyfish to cover bigger distances looking for reasonable prey.

2.3. Arm Roping:

Certain jellyfish utilize a special hunting procedure known as limb roping. Rather than depending entirely on nematocysts for prey catch, these jellyfish utilize their limbs to make an actual rope like design. At the point when prey comes into contact with the arms, the jellyfish gets its chime, fixing the tether and capturing the prey. This methodology is especially compelling in catching bigger or more equivocal organic entities, displaying the variety of savage strategies utilized by various jellyfish species.

2.4. Cnidocyte Receptor Reaction:

The productivity of jellyfish hunting procedures is improved by their capacity to balance their reaction in view of the sort of prey experienced. Cnidocyte receptors, tangible designs on the jellyfish's body, empower them to recognize various upgrades, including the size and development examples of likely prey. This versatile reaction permits jellyfish to upgrade their hunting procedures in light of the particular difficulties introduced by various life forms in their current circumstance.

Influence on Marine Biological systems:

The prey inclinations and hunting systems of jellyfish have significant ramifications for marine environments, affecting trophic collaborations, supplement cycling, and the construction of food networks.

3.1. Trophic Cooperations:

Jellyfish possess different trophic levels in marine food networks, acting both as hunters and prey. By benefiting from planktonic creatures and little fish, jellyfish impact the overflow and circulation of these prey species. At the same time, they act as a food hotspot for bigger hunters, including fish, ocean turtles, and certain seabirds. The trophic collaborations including jellyfish assume a powerful part in molding the construction and working of marine environments.

3.2. Rivalry with Fish:

The prey inclinations of jellyfish, particularly their dependence on planktonic creatures, can prompt contest with fish for comparable food assets. In conditions where both jellyfish and fish are bountiful, contest for planktonic prey might impact the piece and conveyance of fish populaces. Understanding the elements of contest among jellyfish and fish is vital for anticipating the effect of jellyfish on industrially important fish stocks.

3.3. Prey-Interceded Supplement Cycling:

The taking care of and assimilation cycles of jellyfish add to supplement cycling in marine environments. By catching and processing prey, jellyfish discharge supplements once again into the water through discharge and disintegration. This prey-interceded supplement cycling has suggestions for essential efficiency and supplement accessibility in the general climate. Jellyfish sprouts, portrayed by the quick expansion in jellyfish overflow, can altogether impact supplement elements in marine biological systems.

Natural Effects on Prey Inclinations:

Jellyfish prey inclinations are not static; they are impacted by a bunch of ecological variables that shape the accessibility and circulation of prey organic entities in the marine climate.

4.1. Temperature:

Temperature assumes an essential part in impacting jellyfish physiology and, thus, their prey inclinations. Different jellyfish species show temperature inclinations that influence their metabolic rates and in general movement levels. Hotter temperatures might improve the effectiveness of processing and supplement assimilation, possibly impacting the taking care of rates and outcome of jellyfish populaces.

4.2. Supplement Accessibility:

The accessibility of supplements in the water section straightforwardly influences the overflow and circulation of planktonic life forms, an essential part of jellyfish eats less. Supplement rich conditions, for example, those related with upwelling zones or regions with high essential efficiency, give more than adequate food assets to jellyfish. Changes in supplement accessibility, whether normal or anthropogenic, can affect the progress of jellyfish populaces and their prey inclinations.

4.3. Prey Overflow and Structure:

The overflow and organization of prey organic entities in the general climate fundamentally impact jellyfish taking care of conduct. Jellyfish are deft feeders, changing their hunting methodologies in view of the accessibility and sort of prey. Sprouts of tiny fish or other thick life forms can set off expanded taking care of movement, prompting the quick multiplication of jellyfish populaces during specific natural circumstances.

Human Effects and Preservation Contemplations:

Human exercises, going from overfishing to contamination and environmental change, significantly affect jellyfish populaces and their prey inclinations. Understanding these effects is essential for viable protection and the executives methodologies.

5.1. Overfishing and Trophic Fountains:

Overfishing, especially of economically significant fish species, can upset the equilibrium of marine food networks and impact jellyfish populaces. Diminished predation tension on jellyfish prey, joined with the evacuation of contending fish species, may add to the multiplication of jellyfish populaces. This peculiarity, known as a trophic fountain, underscores the interconnected idea of marine biological systems and the requirement for comprehensive administration draws near.

5.2. Eutrophication and Changed Supplement Elements:

Eutrophication, coming about because of the inordinate contribution of supplements into oceanic environments, can affect jellyfish and their prey. Raised supplement levels can animate the development of planktonic living beings, giving plentiful food assets to jellyfish. Also, eutrophication might add to the arrangement of no man's lands, regions with low oxygen levels that might incline toward jellyfish species adjusted to low-oxygen conditions.

5.3. Environmental Change and Sea Warming:

Environmental change, driven by human exercises, adds to climbing ocean temperatures and adjustments in maritime circumstances. These progressions can impact the dissemination, conduct, and prey inclinations of jellyfish. Changes in the timing and power of jellyfish sprouts have been connected to environment related factors, accentuating the need to think about the more extensive biological results of world-wide ecological changes.

Alleviation and The board Procedures:

To address the difficulties presented by jellyfish and their collaborations with marine environments, successful moderation and the executives systems are fundamental.

6.1. Feasible Fisheries The board:

Executing economical fisheries the board rehearses is essential for keeping up with the harmony among jellyfish and industrially important fish stocks. Environment based fisheries the board, which considers the more extensive natural setting, forestalls overfishing and limits the potential for trophic fountains that favor jellyfish.

6.2. Checking and Early Admonition Frameworks:

Checking jellyfish populaces and natural circumstances is fundamental for anticipating and answering potential issues connected with their prey inclinations and taking care of conduct. Early admonition frameworks, upheld by trend setting innovations and information assortment, can give significant data to fisheries, hydroponics activities, and waterfront networks. This empowers convenient and versatile administration techniques to relieve the effect of jellyfish blossoms on human exercises and marine biological systems.

6.3. Incorporated Waterfront Zone The board:

Incorporated Seaside Zone The executives (ICZM) approaches think about the intricate collaborations among jellyfish and their current circumstance inside a more extensive waterfront the board structure. By tending to numerous stressors, including contamination, environment corruption, and overfishing, ICZM advances the feasible utilization of seaside assets and the safeguarding of biological system wellbeing. Such incorporated approaches are significant for dealing with the effects of jellyfish on marine biological systems.

2.3 Relationship with Planktonic Organisms

In the tremendous span of the world's seas, a sensitive dance unfurls among jellyfish and planktonic creatures, molding the elements of marine biological systems. The connection among jellyfish and planktonic living beings is an intricate interchange of predation, contest, and biological transformation. This investigation dives into the complex idea of this relationship, revealing insight into how jellyfish associate with planktonic organic entities and the biological ramifications of these cooperations.

Characterizing Planktonic Creatures:

Prior to digging into the relationship, characterizing planktonic organisms is fundamental. Tiny fish contains a different local area of minute organic entities that float or float in the water section, unfit to swim against the flows. This people group incorporates phytoplankton, the essential makers that do photosynthesis, and zooplankton, which comprises of little creatures that act as a urgent connection in marine food networks.

1.1. Phytoplankton - The Essential Makers:

Phytoplankton, comprising principally of minuscule green growth and cyanobacteria, assume a basic part in marine environments by outfitting daylight to create natural mixtures through photosynthesis. These little, photosynthetic organic entities structure the foundation of the marine food web, giving the energy source to different marine organic entities, including jellyfish.

1.2. Zooplankton - A Different People group:

Zooplankton envelops a different exhibit of little creatures, including copepods, krill, and larval types of different marine life forms. These creatures act as a basic connection between essential makers (phytoplankton) and higher trophic levels in the marine pecking order. Zooplankton, being helpless before sea flows, are profoundly powerless to predation, including that of jellyfish.

Jellyfish Taking care of Variations:

Jellyfish have advanced a variety of taking care of transformations that permit them to catch and consume planktonic life forms proficiently. The connection among jellyfish and planktonic living beings is basically characterized by the hunting systems utilized by jellyfish to explore the immense scope of the vast sea and secure their food.

2.1. Nematocysts and Appendages - Specific Savage Apparatuses:

Fundamental to the taking care of outcome of jellyfish are their specific designs known as nematocysts. Circulated along the outer layer of their limbs, these minute, spear like designs permit jellyfish to catch and immobilize prey. At the point when a jellyfish comes into contact with planktonic creatures, the nematocysts are set off, sending off a quick reaction to catch the floating prey.

2.2. Trap Predation and Limb Float:

Numerous jellyfish species utilize trap predation as an essential hunting procedure. Situated with their appendages expanded, jellyfish stand by without complaining for planktonic organic entities to come into contact with their stinging cells. This latent methodology benefits from the normal float of microscopic fish with sea ebbs and flows, making jellyfish proficient at catching a ceaseless stream of floating organic entities.

2.3. Dynamic Hunting and Swimming Examples:

Some jellyfish species are dynamic trackers, showing ways of behaving, for example, swimming and pursuit to search out and catch planktonic creatures effectively. Their throbbing chime developments impel them through the water, empowering them to cover bigger distances and effectively draw in with their prey. Dynamic hunting methodologies are especially beneficial in conditions where planktonic organic entities are scattered or while experiencing more versatile prey.

2.4. Arm Roping:

An exceptional variation saw in specific jellyfish species is arm roping. Rather than depending entirely on nematocysts for prey catch, these jellyfish utilize their limbs to make an actual tether like construction. By getting their ringer, they fix the tether around planktonic organic entities, capturing them actually. This methodology is particularly compelling in catching bigger or more hesitant prey inside the water segment.

Jellyfish and Phytoplankton Elements:

The connection among jellyfish and phytoplankton is entwined in the perplexing equilibrium of marine biological systems. Jellyfish apply impact over phytoplankton elements through predation and supplement cycling, molding the overflow and circulation of these essential makers.

3.1. Phytoplankton as a Food Source:

While jellyfish are transcendently zooplanktivores, benefiting from zooplankton, hatchlings, and little fish, a few animal categories likewise consume phytoplankton. This happens by implication when jellyfish catch and consume zooplankton that have benefited from phytoplankton. Along these lines, jellyfish add to the progression of energy through the marine food web, affecting both phytoplankton and zooplankton populaces.

3.2. Supplement Cycling and Blossom Elements:

The taking care of and assimilation cycles of jellyfish assume a part in supplement cycling inside marine environments. As jellyfish catch and overview prey, supplements are delivered once again into the water through discharge and disintegration. This supplement reusing can impact phytoplankton elements, possibly adding to the event and constancy of phytoplankton sprouts in specific districts.

3.3. Jellyfish Blossoms and Phytoplankton Reaction:

The connection among jellyfish and phytoplankton turns out to be especially important with regards to jellyfish sprouts. Jellyfish sprouts, described by a quick expansion in jellyfish overflow, can have flowing consequences for phytoplankton elements. Expanded predation on zooplankton by sprouting jellyfish may by implication influence phytoplankton populaces, influencing the equilibrium of the biological system.

Jellyfish and Zooplankton Collaborations:

The mind boggling dance among jellyfish and zooplankton envelops an intricate trap of predation, rivalry, and natural connections. The connection between these two parts of the marine climate has suggestions for the construction and working of marine biological systems.

4.1. Predation on Zooplankton:

Jellyfish are noticeable hunters of zooplankton, going after copepods, krill, and other little creatures that make up the zooplankton local area. The nematocysts on jellyfish arms consider productive catch and immobilization of zooplankton, adding to the energy move through the food web.

4.2. Rivalry for Assets:

The connection among jellyfish and zooplankton includes rivalry for assets, especially phytoplankton. As both jellyfish and zooplankton depend on phytoplankton as an essential food source, changes in the wealth of one gathering can impact the accessibility of assets for the other. Understanding the elements of this opposition is significant for anticipating the effect of jellyfish on zooplankton populaces.

4.3. Trophic Fountains:

Jellyfish predation on zooplankton can have flowing impacts on marine environments, affecting higher trophic levels. By diminishing the overflow of zooplankton, jellyfish may by implication influence the living beings that depend on zooplankton as a food source, like little fish and larval phases of bigger marine species. These trophic fountains feature the interconnected idea of marine food networks.

Natural Elements Impacting Connections:

The connection among jellyfish and planktonic living beings isn't static and is affected by different natural factors that shape the accessibility and conveyance of these life forms in the marine climate.

5.1. Temperature:

Temperature assumes a critical part in impacting the metabolic rates and movement levels of jellyfish and planktonic life forms. Various types of jellyfish and tiny fish have fluctuating temperature inclinations, and changes in ocean temperature can affect their communications. Hotter temperatures might upgrade the productivity of metabolic cycles associated with taking care of and absorption, impacting the general progress of jellyfish populaces.

5.2. Flows and Water Development:

Sea flows and water development assume a critical part in the dissemination of planktonic organic entities and the development of jellyfish. The inactive floating procedure utilized by some jellyfish lines up with the regular development of microscopic fish with sea flows. Changes in current examples can impact the experience rates among jellyfish and planktonic prey, forming the elements of their relationship.

5.3. Supplement Accessibility:

The accessibility of supplements in the water section straightforwardly influences the overflow and dispersion of planktonic creatures, especially phytoplankton. Supplement rich conditions give adequate food assets to both jellyfish and planktonic organic entities, affecting the progress of their populaces. Changes in supplement accessibility, whether regular or anthropogenic, can have flowing consequences for the connection among jellyfish and microscopic fish.

Protection Suggestions and The board Techniques:

Understanding the complexities of the connection among jellyfish and planktonic creatures is vital for successful marine preservation and the board systems. The ramifications of this relationship stretch out past the quick communications between these creatures, affecting more extensive biological system elements.

6.1. Checking and Early Admonition Frameworks:

Checking jellyfish populaces, microscopic fish elements, and natural circumstances is fundamental for anticipating and answering potential issues connected with their relationship. Early admonition frameworks, upheld by headways in innovation and information assortment, can give important data to fisheries, hydroponics tasks, and beach front networks. This empowers ideal and versatile administration techniques to moderate the effect of jellyfish sprouts on marine biological systems.

6.2. Coordinated Biological system The board:

Coordinated biological system the board moves toward that think about the complicated connections between jellyfish, tiny fish, and different parts of marine environments are fundamental. By taking on all encompassing administration procedures, for example, environment based fisheries the executives, we can guarantee the supportability of marine assets and relieve potential disturbances brought about by changes in jellyfish elements.

6.3. Relieving Human Effects:

Human exercises, for example, overfishing, supplement contamination, and environmental change, can impact the connection among jellyfish and planktonic organic entities. Carrying out measures to moderate these human effects, like supportable fisheries the board, lessening supplement overflow, and tending to environmental change, is essential for keeping up with the equilibrium of marine biological systems.

Chapter 3

Reproduction And Life Cycle

Jellyfish, with their elegant throbs and ethereal magnificence, harbor a daily existence cycle that is basically as multifaceted as their developments in the sea flows. Propagation is a crucial part of their reality, driving the propagation of these thick organic entities across ages. This investigation dives into the interesting universe of jellyfish proliferation and life cycles, unwinding the stages and components that add to the cryptic expressive dance of life underneath the sea's surface.

Essential Life structures for Proliferation:

Prior to diving into the particulars of jellyfish proliferation, it's fundamental to comprehend the essential life structures that works with this interaction.

1.1. Ringer and Arms:

The ringer, or medusa, is the umbrella-formed body of the jellyfish, normally straightforward and thick. Dangling from the ringer are arms furnished with specific stinging cells called nematocysts. These designs assume pivotal parts in both hunting and generation.

1.2. Manubrium and Balls:

Suspended underneath the chime is the manubrium, a rounded design that fills in as the jellyfish's mouth. Associated with the manubrium are balls, the regenerative organs liable for creating gametes (sperm and eggs). The balls are many times noticeable as spiral waterways reaching out from the focal point of the ringer.

Life Cycle Outline:

Jellyfish display a perplexing life cycle including rotating ages of polyps and medusae. This peculiarity, known as metagenesis or rotation of ages, is an unmistakable element of numerous cnidarians, the phylum to which jellyfish have a place.

2.1. Polyp Stage:

The existence cycle starts with a little, sessile polyp, frequently alluded to as a "scyphistoma." The polyp joins itself to a substrate, for example, rocks or the sea floor, utilizing a tacky basal plate. From the highest point of the polyp, a cylindrical construction known as a "stolon" may expand, interfacing different polyps. The polyp stage is basically described by abiogenetic proliferation through growing.

2.2. Ephyrae Arrangement:

As the polyp develops, it goes through an interaction called "strobilation." During strobilation, the polyp goes through cross over parting, creating piles of circle like designs called ephyrae. These ephyrae in the end separate from the polyp, turning out to be free-swimming adolescent jellyfish.

2.3. Medusa Stage:

The ephyrae form into medusae, the recognizable umbrella-molded jellyfish that cross the vast sea. Medusae are the physically regenerative phase of the jellyfish life cycle, and it is during this stage that sexual generation happens. Once adult, medusae discharge eggs and sperm into the water, starting the treatment interaction.

Sexual Multiplication:

Sexual multiplication in jellyfish is a critical part of their life cycle and happens solely during the medusa stage. This cycle includes the combination of male and female gametes, bringing about the arrangement of a zygote that forms into a planula hatchling.

3.1. Treatment in the Water Section:

In the water segment, male and female jellyfish discharge their gametes at the same time. The sperm and eggs, released into the encompassing water, go through outer preparation. This system improves the possibilities of effective treatment, permitting the blending of hereditary material in the immense region of the vast sea.

3.2. Planula Hatchlings Arrangement:

The prepared egg forms into a planula hatchling, a minuscule, ciliated living being that floats with sea flows. The planula hatchling addresses a momentary stage between the medusa and polyp stages. Its process might require days to weeks, contingent upon ecological circumstances.

Polyp Arrangement and Agamic Multiplication:

After arriving at a reasonable substrate, the planula hatchling goes through transformation, changing into a polyp. This change denotes the fruition of the existence cycle's most memorable stage and starts the agamic proliferation normal for the polyp stage.

4.1. Abiogenetic Growing:

The polyp starts to imitate agamically through an interaction known as growing. Maturing includes the arrangement of hereditarily indistinguishable clones of the first polyp. These clones, called "ephyra buds," form into heaps of ephyrae, each equipped for disengaging and developing into a free-swimming medusa.

4.2. Strobilation:

The sprouting system is joined by strobilation, during which the polyp goes through cross over splitting, making a progression of ephyrae stacked like coins. The ephyrae at last break free, initiating their autonomous presence as adolescent medusae.

Biological Meaning of Rotation of Ages:

The variation of ages in the jellyfish life cycle holds biological importance, adding to the versatility and strength of jellyfish populaces in assorted marine conditions.

5.1. Hereditary Variety:

Variation of ages presents a degree of hereditary variety inside jellyfish populaces. While agamic multiplication during the polyp stage brings about hereditary clones, sexual proliferation during the medusa stage presents inconstancy by rearranging hereditary material through preparation. This hereditary variety upgrades the capacity of jellyfish populaces to adjust to changing ecological circumstances.

5.2. Life Cycle Adaptability:

The presence of both abiogenetic and sexual generation in the existence cycle gives jellyfish a level of adaptability in answering ecological signals. Contingent upon the accessibility of assets, ecological circumstances, and different elements, jellyfish can change the harmony among agamic and sexual generation to boost their regenerative achievement.

Natural Variables Affecting Multiplication:

Jellyfish proliferation is impacted by different natural variables, including temperature, supplement accessibility, and other environmental prompts that shape the outcome of every life cycle stage.

6.1. Temperature:

Temperature assumes a basic part in the timing and progress of jellyfish generation. Various types of jellyfish have explicit temperature ranges for ideal propagation. Hotter temperatures can speed up the advancement of hatchlings and medusae, affecting the planning of jellyfish blossoms and their general overflow in specific districts.

6.2. Supplement Accessibility:

Supplement accessibility in the water section impacts the progress of both larval turn of events and the development of polyps. Higher supplement levels can upgrade the development and conceptive result of polyps, adding to the arrangement of bigger populaces of ephyrae and medusae. Supplement rich circumstances, frequently connected with human exercises like supplement spillover, might possibly fuel jellyfish sprouts.

6.3. Light and Photoperiod:

Light circumstances and the photoperiod (length of sunshine) likewise assume a part in jellyfish propagation. Light signals are fundamental for the settlement of planula hatchlings, directing them to appropriate substrates for polyp connection. Changes in light circumstances might impact the planning of strobilation and ephyra discharge, influencing the elements of jellyfish populaces.

Worldwide Conveyance and Obtrusive Species:

Understanding jellyfish multiplication is essential for anticipating their worldwide dissemination and the potential for specific species to become obtrusive in new conditions.

7.1. Versatility to Various Conditions:

The shift of ages in the jellyfish life cycle improves their versatility to various marine conditions. Polyps, with their agamic conceptive procedure, can flourish in steady, supplement rich circumstances. Interestingly, the medusa stage, with its sexual proliferation, considers hereditary blending and transformation to changing natural circumstances, working with the colonization of assorted territories.

7.2. Weight Water Transport:

Human exercises, like delivery, can accidentally ship jellyfish and their regenerative stages across tremendous distances. Medusae or planula hatchlings present in weight water released from boats can lay out new populaces in districts where they were not initially present. This transport system has added to the presentation of specific jellyfish species into non-local conditions, prompting worries about the expected intrusiveness of these species.

7.3. Environmental Change Effects:

Environmental change, with its related modifications in ocean temperature and maritime circumstances, may impact the appropriation and regenerative examples of jellyfish. Changes in temperature systems could affect the planning of generation, larval turn of events, and the general progress of jellyfish populaces. These potential movements have suggestions for marine biological systems and human exercises subject to seaside and marine assets.

Protection and The board Contemplations:

As jellyfish populaces keep on catching logical and public consideration, contemplations for protection and the board become progressively significant. Understanding the complexities of jellyfish propagation is indispensable to creating successful methodologies for moderating likely adverse consequences.

8.1. Observing and Early Identification:

Ceaseless checking of jellyfish populaces, particularly during key life cycle stages, is vital for early location of populace increments or changes in dissemination. Early identification considers convenient reactions and the execution of the board measures to forestall or alleviate expected environmental and financial effects.

8.2. Incorporated Waterfront Zone The board:

Coordinated Waterfront Zone The executives (ICZM) approaches that consider the perplexing collaborations among jellyfish and their current circumstance are fundamental. By tending to different stressors, including contamination, overfishing, and environment debasement, ICZM advances the manageable utilization of waterfront assets and keeps up with the harmony among jellyfish and different parts of marine biological systems.

8.3. Relieving Anthropogenic Impacts:

Relieving anthropogenic impacts, for example, supplement contamination and environmental change, is fundamental for limiting the expected adverse consequences of jellyfish blossoms. Carrying out measures to lessen supplement spillover, advance economical fisheries the executives, and address environmental change adds to the general strength of marine biological systems and forestalls conditions leaning toward jellyfish multiplication.

3.1 Reproductive Strategies: Sexual and Asexual

The existence of a jellyfish is a hypnotizing dance that unfurls through unpredictable regenerative methodologies. Multiplication is a central part of their reality, and jellyfish utilize a blend of sexual and abiogenetic systems to guarantee the continuation of their genealogy. This investigation digs into the captivating universe of jellyfish regenerative methodologies, unwinding the subtleties of both sexual and abiogenetic systems that add to the versatility and flexibility of these confounding animals.

Sexual Generation: The Medusa Stage Artful dance:

Jellyfish sexual generation becomes the dominant focal point during the medusa period of their life cycle. This stage, portrayed by the natural umbrella-formed ringer and following appendages, is the free-swimming and physically mature phase of jellyfish.

1.1. Arrival of Gametes:

Sexual multiplication in jellyfish includes the arrival of particular conceptive cells known as gametes. Male jellyfish discharge sperm into the water, while females discharge eggs. This synchronized delivery frequently happens during explicit ecological circumstances or triggers, amplifying the possibilities of effective preparation in the huge span of the untamed sea.

1.2. Outside Treatment:

Preparation happens remotely, with the sperm and eggs joining in the water segment. This outside treatment system considers the blending of hereditary material in a cycle that can be impacted by elements like water temperature, flows, and other natural signals. The subsequent zygote forms into a planula hatchling, denoting the beginning of the following stage in the jellyfish life cycle.

1.3. Planula Hatchlings: The Vagabonds of the Sea:

The planula hatchling is a minute, ciliated life form that floats with sea flows. Its process might endure from days to weeks, during which it is conveyed to various areas. The planula hatchling addresses a crucial connection between the medusa and polyp stages, as it chooses a reasonable substrate and goes through transformation into a polyp.

1.4. Hereditary Variety and Flexibility:

Sexual propagation presents hereditary variety inside jellyfish populaces. The rearranging of hereditary material through the mix of various people's gametes improves versatility to changing ecological circumstances. This variety is pivotal for the endurance and outcome of jellyfish populaces in unique marine biological systems.

Abiogenetic Multiplication: The Polyp Stage Ensemble:

While the medusa stage exhibits the class of sexual generation, the polyp stage is an ensemble of agamic procedures. The polyp, a sessile and tube-like design, secures itself to a substrate and goes through cycles, for example, growing and strobilation to multiply.

2.1. Sprouting: Clones as one:

Abiogenetic propagation in the polyp stage fundamentally includes growing. The polyp frames hereditarily indistinguishable clones of itself through the development of new people, frequently alluded to as "ephyra buds." These buds form into piles of ephyrae, each equipped for isolating and developing into free-swimming medusae. The hereditary character of these clones is safeguarded, adding to the arrangement of hereditarily uniform populaces.

2.2. Strobilation: The Craft of Cross over Parting:

Strobilation is a critical cycle in the abiogenetic proliferation of jellyfish during the polyp stage. It includes the cross over splitting of the polyp, bringing about the creation of stacked plate like designs known as ephyrae. These ephyrae in the long run disengage from the polyp, starting their free presence as adolescent medusae. Strobilation considers the quick augmentation of jellyfish populaces.

2.3. Provincial Polyps and Constant Sprouting:

Some jellyfish species display frontier polyps, where various polyps are associated by an organization of stolons. This interconnected design takes into account nonstop growing and the development of new polyps. Pilgrim polyps make bigger and stronger jellyfish populaces, upgrading their capacity to take advantage of positive ecological circumstances.

Joined Methodologies: The Cooperative Dance of Sexual and Agamic Propagation:

Jellyfish organize a complicated expressive dance of life via flawlessly coordinating both sexual and abiogenetic regenerative methodologies. The rotation of ages, where polyps produce medusae and medusae produce polyps, makes a dynamic and versatile life cycle that answers natural signs.

3.1. Metagenesis: The Dance of Ages:

The variation of ages, otherwise called metagenesis, is a sign of numerous cnidarians, including jellyfish. It includes the change between the sessile polyp and the free-swimming medusa stages. This repeating dance permits jellyfish to benefit from the qualities of both conceptive procedures, cultivating hereditary variety and versatility.

3.2. Life Cycle Adaptability:

The coordination of sexual and agamic multiplication gives jellyfish a level of adaptability in their life cycle. Contingent upon natural circumstances, asset accessibility, and different variables, jellyfish can change the harmony among sexual and abiogenetic generation to advance their conceptive achievement. This adaptability adds to their capacity to flourish in different marine conditions.

Environmental Ramifications: Difficult exercises in Marine Biological systems:

The conceptive techniques of jellyfish have significant natural ramifications, impacting the elements of marine biological systems and forming associations with different organic entities.

4.1. Populace Elements and Sprouts:

The joined regenerative systems of jellyfish add to their true capacity for populace blasts, known as blossoms. Abiogenetic propagation during the polyp stage considers the fast increase of people, while sexual proliferation presents hereditary variety.

Sprouts can have flowing consequences for marine biological systems, affecting food networks and contending with different organic entities for assets.

4.2. Trophic Collaborations:

The rotation of ages in jellyfish life cycles impacts trophic collaborations in marine biological systems. As medusae feed on zooplankton and little fish, they add to energy courses through the food web. The expansion of jellyfish populaces, particularly during blossoms, can adjust trophic communications and possibly influence higher trophic levels.

4.3. Biological system Strength and Flexibility:

The flexibility of jellyfish conceptive systems upgrades the strength of marine environments. Because of ecological changes or unsettling influences, jellyfish populaces can change the harmony among sexual and agamic proliferation. This versatility permits them to take advantage of ideal circumstances and bounce back from annoyances, impacting the general elements of marine environments.

Protection Contemplations: Exploring the Regenerative Orchestra:

Understanding the complexities of jellyfish conceptive techniques is essential for preservation endeavors and reasonable marine administration. The likely effects of jellyfish blossoms on environments and human exercises require insightful ways to deal with conjunction.

5.1. Checking and Early Discovery:

Consistent observing of jellyfish populaces, particularly during key phases of their life cycle, is fundamental for early identification of blossoms and populace shifts. Early location empowers convenient reactions and the execution of the executives measures to moderate expected environmental and monetary effects.

5.2. Coordinated Environment The board:

Coordinated Biological system The executives (IEM) approaches that consider the complicated cooperations among jellyfish and their current circumstance are critical. By tending to numerous stressors, including contamination, overfishing, and environment debasement, IEM advances the supportable utilization of waterfront assets and keeps up with the harmony among jellyfish and different parts of marine biological systems.

5.3. Public Mindfulness and Schooling:

Raising public mindfulness about jellyfish science and the environmental job they play is fundamental. Teaching people group about the variables affecting jellyfish sprouts, their likely effects, and the significance of manageable beach front practices encourages understanding and participation in dealing with these perplexing marine organic entities.

3.2 Role of Polyps in the Life Cycle

In the hypnotizing artful dance of life underneath the sea's surface, jellyfish arise as ethereal artists, smoothly exploring the flows. At the core of this unpredictable dance lies the baffling job of polyps, the frequently ignored draftsmen of the jellyfish life cycle. Polyps, the sessile and tube-like designs, assume an essential part in coordinating the rotation of ages, driving the changes between the fixed polyp stage and the free-swimming medusa stage. This investigation dives into the diverse job of polyps in the jellyfish life cycle, disentangling their commitments to the flexibility, strength, and biological meaning of these thick animals.

Polyps as the Fundamental Stage:

The existence pattern of jellyfish starts with the polyp, an apparently unpretentious design that secures itself to a substrate, going from rocks to the sea floor. This sessile stage, otherwise called the scyphistoma, marks the start of the mind boggling advantageous interaction among polyps and the marine climate.

1.1. Connection and Stationary Way of life:

Polyps join themselves to substrates utilizing a tacky basal circle, getting a steady place that permits them to endure the recurring pattern of sea flows. This connection is a basic transformation that works with their stationary way of life, filling in as the establishment for the resulting periods of the jellyfish life cycle.

1.2. Stolon Arrangement: Organized Polyps:

In some jellyfish species, polyps broaden their impact through the development of stolons, which are level designs associating various polyps. This interconnected organization of polyps improves their aggregate conceptive potential and versatility, making an establishment for the expansion of ephyrae and medusae.

1.3. Abiogenetic Multiplication: The Bud Orchestra:

A huge commitment of polyps to the jellyfish life cycle is their part in agamic multiplication. Through a cycle known as growing, polyps lead to hereditarily indistinguishable clones, shaping heaps of ephyra buds. This agamic generation takes into consideration the quick increase of jellyfish people and lays the preparation for the resulting medusa stage.

Strobilation: Polyps as Transformative Engineers:

The extraordinary course of strobilation denotes a critical stage in the existence cycle, where polyps go through a transformative change, making way for the development of adolescent medusae.

2.1. Cross over Parting: Making Ephyrae:

Strobilation includes the momentous peculiarity of cross over parting, where the polyp goes through division into stacked, circle like designs known as ephyrae. These ephyrae act as the adolescent types of medusae and ultimately confine from the polyp, setting out on their autonomous excursion through the water segment.

2.2. Synchronization and Timing: Natural Triggers:

The course of strobilation is many times impacted by natural signals like temperature, light, and supplement accessibility. Polyps display a surprising skill to synchronize strobilation, guaranteeing that ephyrae are delivered into the water segment under conditions helpful for their endurance and resulting development into medusae.

Provincial Polyps: An Orchestra of Participation:

Some jellyfish species show a provincial way of life, where numerous polyps are associated by stolons, shaping a helpful organization of interconnected people.

3.1. Consistent Maturing and Multiplication:

Pioneer polyps participate in constant maturing, making a continuous ensemble of abiogenetic generation. The interconnected idea of pilgrim polyps considers a cooperative exertion in multiplication, with every polyp adding to the expansion of ephyrae and the ensuing age of medusae.

3.2. Improved Versatility and Flexibility:

The pioneer way of life of interconnected polyps improves the versatility and flexibility of jellyfish populaces. It considers aggregate reactions to natural changes, with the possibility to take advantage of great circumstances and climate annoyances. Provincial polyps epitomize the helpful soul implanted in the engineering of the jelly-fish life cycle.

Commitment to Hereditary Variety: The Medusa-Polyp Tango:

The variation of ages, a sign of numerous cnidarians including jellyfish, includes a dance between the medusa and polyp stages. This musical rotation adds to hereditary variety, a urgent calculate the flexibility and transformative progress of jellyfish populaces.

4.1. Hereditary Blending Through Sexual Propagation:

The medusa stage addresses the physically adult period of the jellyfish life cycle. During this stage, medusae discharge gametes into the water, prompting outer treatment. The subsequent planula hatchlings go through transformation into polyps, denoting the commencement of the future. The coordination of sexual multiplication presents hereditary inconstancy, improving the versatility of jellyfish populaces.

4.2. Adjusting Hereditary Consistency and Variety:

The mix of abiogenetic generation by polyps and sexual multiplication by medusae makes a fragile harmony between hereditary consistency and variety. While abiogenetic generation prompts the development of hereditarily indistinguishable clones, sexual multiplication presents inconstancy. This dance among consistency and variety gives jellyfish populaces the devices to flourish in a powerful marine climate.

Polyps and Ecological Transformations:

Polyps are instrumental in interceding the flexibility of jellyfish to changing ecological circumstances. Their capacity to answer signs and triggers guarantees that ensuing ages are delivered into the water section under ideal conditions.

5.1. Temperature Awareness:

The planning of key occasions in the jellyfish life cycle, including strobilation, is frequently impacted by temperature. Polyps show aversion to temperature vacillations, synchronizing the arrival of ephyrae during periods when ecological circumstances are helpful for the endurance and development of adolescent medusae.

5.2. Light and Photoperiod:

Light circumstances and the photoperiod assume a part in the settlement of planula hatchlings and the commencement of strobilation. Polyps answer light signals, guaranteeing that the arrival of ephyrae lines up with ideal ecological circumstances. Changes in light accessibility can impact the timing and progress of key life cycle occasions.

5.3. Supplement Accessibility:

Polyps are receptive to supplement accessibility in their environmental elements, impacting their development, proliferation, and the general progress of the jellyfish life cycle. Supplement rich conditions support the advancement of polyps and add to the arrangement of bigger populaces of ephyrae and medusae.

Biological system Suggestions: Polyps as Modelers of Equilibrium:

The job of polyps reaches out past the bounds of their singular designs, forming the elements of marine biological systems and affecting trophic connections.

6.1. Populace Elements and Trophic Associations:

The multiplication of polyps through abiogenetic generation adds to the potential for jellyfish sprouts. As medusae feed on zooplankton and little fish, the overflow of polyps and medusae can impact trophic communications, affecting higher trophic levels in marine biological systems.

6.2. Asset Contest:

Polyps and medusae seek assets, especially phytoplankton and zooplankton. The outcome of polyps in a given climate can impact the overflow and conveyance of resulting medusae, adding to the general equilibrium of asset usage inside marine biological systems.

6.3. Environment Versatility:

The versatility of jellyfish populaces, driven to a limited extent by the job of polyps, upgrades the strength of marine biological systems. In light of ecological changes or aggravations, jellyfish can change the harmony among sexual and abiogenetic proliferation, adding to the soundness and versatility of marine environments.

Preservation Suggestions: Exploring the Polyp-Medusa Tango:

Understanding the essential job of polyps in the jellyfish life cycle has critical ramifications for protection endeavors and the supportable administration of marine biological systems.

7.1. Checking Polyp Populaces:

Constant checking of polyp populaces, particularly in regions inclined to jellyfish sprouts, is urgent for figuring out the potential for ensuing medusa expansion. Checking polyp overflow and conceptive movement gives experiences into the elements impacting jellyfish elements and considers early identification of movements in populace elements.

7.2. Incorporated Biological system The executives:

Incorporated Biological system The executives (IEM) approaches that think about the perplexing connections between polyps, medusae, and their current circumstance are fundamental. By tending to numerous stressors, including contamination, overfishing, and living space debasement, IEM advances the reasonable utilization of beach front assets and keeps up with the harmony among jellyfish and different parts of marine biological systems.

7.3. Relieving Anthropogenic Impacts:

Human exercises, for example, supplement contamination and environmental change, can affect the progress of polyps and the general elements of the jellyfish life cycle. Carrying out measures to relieve these anthropogenic impacts, for example, decreasing supplement overflow and tending to environmental change, is vital for keeping up with the equilibrium of marine biological systems.

3.3 Environmental Factors Influencing Reproduction

Life underneath the sea's surface is a dynamic and complex embroidery molded by a heap of natural variables. Proliferation, a key part of the endurance and propagation of marine living beings, is profoundly impacted by the circumstances and signs given by the general climate. This investigation dives into the broad domain of natural factors that assume an essential part in impacting multiplication in marine organic entities. From temperature and supplement accessibility to light and occasional changes, each variable adds to the fragile equilibrium of life in the oceanic domains.

Temperature: The Thermodynamic Ensemble:

Temperature remains as an expert director in the coordination of marine generation, impacting the timing, achievement, and techniques took on by different creatures.

1.1. Warm Resistance and Ideal Reaches:

Different marine species show explicit warm resiliences and ideal temperature ranges for multiplication. For the vast majority marine creatures, temperature changes outside these reaches can disturb conceptive cycles. Hotter temperatures frequently speed up metabolic rates and formative cycles, affecting the planning of regenerative occasions.

1.2. Occasional Timing of Multiplication:

Occasional changes in temperature assume an essential part in the planning of propagation for various marine species. Numerous creatures synchronize their regenerative cycles with occasional temperature designs, guaranteeing that hatchlings or posterity are delivered during periods when natural circumstances are helpful for their endurance.

1.3. Effect of Environmental Change:

Environmental change, with its related climb in ocean temperatures, has significant ramifications for marine multiplication. Changes in temperature systems can adjust the timing and outcome of conceptive occasions, possibly prompting befuddles between the accessibility of assets and the regenerative necessities of marine organic entities.

Supplement Accessibility: Treating the Sea Nurseries:

Supplement accessibility in marine environments fills in as a vital determinant of regenerative achievement, impacting the development, improvement, and generally wellbeing of creatures.

2.1. Supplement Rich Conditions:

Seaside regions frequently experience higher supplement focuses because of elements like upwelling, stream spillover, and anthropogenic data sources. These supplement rich conditions make ripe reason for the expansion of phytoplankton, framing the foundation of the marine food web and giving fundamental supplements to regenerative cycles.

2.2. Eutrophication and Algal Blossoms:

Inordinate supplement input, frequently connected with human exercises, for example, rural overflow and wastewater release, can prompt eutrophication. While eutrophication can set off destructive algal sprouts, it can likewise fuel the development of phytoplankton, supporting the propagation of channel taking care of living beings and adding to the outcome of larval stages.

2.3. Restricting Supplements: Iron and Micronutrients:

In specific locales, the accessibility of explicit micronutrients, like iron, can restrict conceptive achievement. Iron is a critical part for phytoplankton development, and its shortage in a few marine conditions might impact the general efficiency of biological systems and the creatures reliant upon them.

Light and Photoperiod: Enlightening Regenerative Pathways:

Light, a central ecological variable, fills in as a reference point directing the conceptive pathways of marine living beings. Photoperiod, the term of sunshine, impacts the planning of regenerative occasions and the way of behaving of different species.

3.1. Photoperiod as an Occasional Prompt:

Changes in day length all through the year go about as occasional prompts for the overwhelming majority marine organic entities. Photoperiod triggers the inception of conceptive cycles, affecting the planning of gamete discharge, larval turn of events, and other basic regenerative occasions.

3.2. Light in Coral Generation:

Light is a fundamental consider the conceptive systems of coral reefs. A few coral animal categories show simultaneous generating occasions set off by lunar cycles, with the arrival of eggs and sperm happening during explicit periods of the moon. Light additionally impacts the settlement and transformation of coral hatchlings.

3.3. Remote ocean Variations:

In the remote ocean climate, where daylight entrance is negligible, bioluminescence turns into a significant calculate regenerative way of behaving. Some remote ocean creatures utilize bioluminescent presentations for correspondence, mate fascination, and possibly as a system to synchronize regenerative exercises without a trace of daylight.

Saltiness and Osmoregulation: Exploring the Harsh Waters:

Saltiness, the grouping of disintegrated salts in water, impacts the osmoregulatory challenges looked by marine life forms. Changes in saltiness can affect the conceptive progress of species adjusted to explicit reaches.

4.1. Estuarine and Harsh Conditions:

Estuarine conditions, described by fluctuating saltiness levels, present difficulties and potential open doors for conceptive achievement. A few marine animal groups have adjusted to harsh waters, where they might encounter varieties in saltiness because of flowing vacillations and freshwater input from waterways.

4.2. Anadromous and Catadromous Fish:

Anadromous and catadromous fish species, which relocate among freshwater and marine conditions for multiplication, are especially delicate to saltiness changes. The planning of their movements and the outcome of bringing forth occasions are complicatedly connected to saltiness slopes in estuaries and waterway mouths.

4.3. Osmoregulation in Marine Spineless creatures:

Marine spineless creatures, including shellfish and mollusks, are exceptionally delicate to changes in saltiness. Osmoregulation, the guideline of interior water and salt equilibrium, is pivotal for their endurance and regenerative achievement. Variances in saltiness can affect larval turn of events and in general conceptive wellbeing.

Flows and Oceanography: Exploring the Progression of Life:

Sea flows and the actual qualities of the marine climate impact the dispersal of gametes and hatchlings, forming the network and hereditary variety of marine populaces.

5.1. Dispersal of Gametes and Hatchlings:

The development of sea flows assumes a vital part in the dispersal of gametes and hatchlings. For the vast majority marine creatures, the capacity to deliver regenerative components decisively into flows improves the possibilities of effective preparation and the colonization of new natural surroundings.

5.2. Availability and Hereditary Variety:

Sea flows add to the availability of marine populaces, affecting the trading of hereditary material between far off areas. High availability upgrades hereditary variety, permitting populaces to adjust to changing natural circumstances and advancing flexibility despite aggravations.

5.3. Upwelling and Supplement Supply:

Upwelling, the vertical development of supplement rich profound water to the surface, impacts the efficiency of marine biological systems. Regions encountering upwelling are described by upgraded supplement supply, which can invigorate phytoplankton development and make good circumstances for the multiplication of channel taking care of creatures.

pH and Sea Fermentation: Exploring the Acidic Oceans:

The pH of seawater, a proportion of its sharpness or alkalinity, is a basic ecological variable that has collected expanding consideration because of sea fermentation coming about because of raised carbon dioxide (CO_2) levels.

6.1. Influence on Calcifying Living beings:

Sea fermentation presents difficulties to marine organic entities, especially those that depend on calcium carbonate for the arrangement of shells and skeletons. Calcifying living beings like mollusks, corals, and a few planktonic animal groups might encounter decreased conceptive accomplishment because of changes in pH.

6.2. Suggestions for Fish Multiplication:

Fish multiplication can be affected by changes in pH, with likely impacts on egg advancement, larval endurance, and the general progress of producing occasions.

Aversion to pH changes differs among species, featuring the requirement for species-explicit appraisals even with sea fermentation.

6.3. Variations and Developmental Reactions:

A few marine life forms might display versatile reactions or developmental changes because of sea fermentation. Understanding the limit of species to adapt or develop notwithstanding changing pH conditions is significant for anticipating the drawn out influences on regenerative achievement.

Occasional and Environment Driven Changeability: The Dance of Earth's Rhythms:

Occasional and environment driven changeability in ecological variables, like temperature, precipitation, and barometrical examples, can altogether impact conceptive cycles in marine creatures.

7.1. El Niño and La Niña Occasions:

Climatic peculiarities like El Niño and La Niña occasions can impact sea temperatures and flows, disturbing common natural circumstances. These occasions can affect the timing and outcome of generation, prompting shifts in the circulation and overflow of marine species.

7.2. Rainstorm and Precipitation:

In seaside areas impacted by rainstorm, occasional changes in precipitation can influence saltiness levels, supplement inputs, and the general efficiency of marine environments. These progressions can, thusly, impact the conceptive way of behaving and outcome of creatures adjusted to these unique conditions.

7.3. Long haul Environment Patterns:

The drawn out patterns related with environmental change, for example, climbing temperatures and ocean level, can apply progressive however relentless impacts on marine generation. Understanding the combined effects of environmental change on conceptive cycles is significant for anticipating future changes in marine biological systems.

Anthropogenic Impacts: The Human Impression on Proliferation:

Human exercises, from contamination to overfishing, present extra stressors that can disturb the fragile equilibrium of marine propagation.

8.1. Contamination and Endocrine Interruption:

Contamination from agrarian spillover, modern releases, and plastic flotsam and jetsam brings impurities into marine conditions. These contaminations can disturb endocrine frameworks in marine organic entities, influencing regenerative chemicals and cycles.

8.2. Overfishing and Asset Exhaustion:

Overfishing can exhaust populaces of target species, disturbing the equilibrium of marine biological systems and influencing the regenerative outcome of impacted species. The expulsion of key hunters or contenders can have flowing consequences for the overflow and conduct of different creatures in the biological system.

8.3. Territory Annihilation and Seaside Advancement:

Territory annihilation coming about because of seaside advancement, digging, and other human exercises can straightforwardly influence the accessibility of appropriate natural surroundings for generation. Loss of basic favorable places and settling destinations can prompt decreases in regenerative accomplishment for different marine species.

Chapter 4

Environmental Adaptations

Natural transformations allude to the changes and adjustments that living organic entities go through to adapt to changes in their environmental factors. These variations are fundamental for endurance, permitting organic entities to flourish in assorted and frequently testing biological systems. Whether ashore, in water, or in the air, creatures have advanced more than huge number of years to foster characteristics and ways of behaving that increment their possibilities of endurance and generation in their particular surroundings.

Transformative Groundworks of Natural Variations

The idea of ecological transformation is well established in the standards of advancement. Charles Darwin's hypothesis of normal determination, illustrated in his fundamental work "On the Beginning of Species," gives a thorough system to understanding how species adjust to their surroundings over progressive ages. As per Darwin, people inside a populace show variety in characteristics, and those qualities that present an endurance advantage are bound to be given to the future.

After some time, this cycle prompts the gathering of helpful characteristics inside a populace, bringing about transformations that upgrade the wellness of people in their particular surroundings. Natural transformations can happen at different levels, including physical, physiological, social, and biological, and they are molded by the particular difficulties and open doors introduced by a specific environment.

Physical Transformations

Physical transformations include primary changes in the body of a life form to more readily suit its current circumstance. These variations can be seen in different parts of an organic entity's life structures, for example, its body shape, extremities, and inward organs.

Model: Disguise in the Animals of the world collectively

Disguise is a predominant physical transformation seen in numerous species across the animals of the world collectively. The capacity to mix into the general climate gives a pivotal benefit in keeping away from hunters or upgrading hunting achievement.

For example, the peppered moth (Biston betularia) in Britain created different variety varieties that permitted it to more readily match the bark of trees during the Modern Transformation, when contamination obscured the tree trunks.

Likewise, the leaf-followed gecko (Uroplatus phantasticus) of Madagascar has developed to look like a dead leaf, complete with sporadic edges and tinge that reflects the encompassing foliage. These variations feature the complex manners by which organic entities have advanced to take advantage of their environments for endurance.

Physiological Variations

Physiological variations include changes in the inside working of a creature, like metabolic cycles, biochemical pathways, or other physiological systems. These transformations empower living beings to carry out fundamental roles all the more productively because of explicit ecological difficulties.

Model: Thermoregulation in Desert Creatures

Desert conditions are portrayed by outrageous temperature changes, with singing intensity during the day and cold temperatures around evening time. Desert-abiding creatures, for example, the fennec fox (Vulpes zerda) and the camel (Camelus spp.), have created effective physiological instruments for thermoregulation.

Fennec foxes, with their enormous ears, can disseminate heat all the more successfully through expanded surface region, while camels can manage their internal heat level over a wide reach, permitting them to endure the unforgiving states of the desert. These physiological variations are fundamental for keeping up with interior equilibrium and forestalling heat-related pressure in these parched conditions.

Conduct Variations

Conduct variations include changes in an organic entity's way of behaving to more readily suit its current circumstance. These transformations are frequently educated or instinctual reactions to natural prompts and difficulties.

Model: Relocation in Birds

Movement is a far reaching conduct transformation saw in many bird species. Birds, like the Cold tern (Sterna paradisaea), attempt significant distance ventures among rearing and wintering grounds to take advantage of occasional varieties in asset accessibility. This conduct permits them to get to bountiful food sources, stay away from brutal atmospheric conditions, and increment their possibilities of endurance and conceptive achievement.

Relocation is an intricate way of behaving that includes inborn impulses, gaining for a fact, and ecological prompts like day length and temperature. The capacity to explore across tremendous distances is a noteworthy illustration of how conduct transformations add to the endurance of species in powerful and geologically different conditions.

Environmental Transformations

Natural transformations include the collaborations among organic entities and their surroundings at the local area and biological system levels. These transformations impact the conveyance and wealth of species in various natural surroundings.

Model: Hydrophytic Variations in Amphibian Plants

Sea-going plants show a scope of biological transformations to flourish in water-logged conditions. Hydrophytic transformations incorporate highlights like particular root foundations, decreased fingernail skin thickness, and the presence of aerenchyma tissue, which works with gas trade in lowered plant parts.

Water lilies (Nymphaea spp.) are a magnificent illustration of hydrophytic variations. Their leaves have a waxy surface that repulses water, forestalling submersion, and stomata on the upper leaf surface take into consideration gas trade. Moreover, the foundations of amphibian plants are adjusted to extricate supplements from the water, featuring how natural variations add to the outcome of plants in sea-going biological systems.

Human Natural Variations

People, as an animal categories, have likewise gone through huge natural transformations all through their developmental history. From the advancement of hardware use to the foundation of farming practices, people have consistently adjusted to their environmental elements to address their issues and beat difficulties.

Model: Social Variations to Environment

Human social orders have created different social variations because of climatic circumstances. For instance, the Inuit nation of the Cold have customarily depended on ice fishing, hunting marine vertebrates, and building protected abodes to get by in freezing temperatures. Interestingly, the Maasai nation of East Africa have adjusted to the semi-bone-dry savannah by rehearsing migrant pastoralism, moving their domesticated animals to regions with accessible brushing and water.

These social transformations include a blend of information, practices, and social designs that empower human populaces to flourish in different natural settings. As innovation and globalization keep on propelling, understanding and safeguarding these social transformations become pivotal for economical concurrence with the climate.

Contemporary Difficulties and Transformations

Even with continuous ecological changes driven by human exercises, life forms are confronting new and exceptional difficulties. Environmental change, territory annihilation, contamination, and other anthropogenic impacts are adjusting the normal scenes and biological systems that life forms have adjusted to over centuries. Thus, a few animal categories are battling to adapt to quickly evolving conditions.

Model: Polar Bear Transformations to Dissolving Ocean Ice

Polar bears (Ursus maritimus) are famous occupants of the Cold, depending on ocean ice as a stage for hunting seals. In any case, the liquefying of Icy ocean ice because of an unnatural weather change presents a huge test for these bears. As the ice subsides, polar bears should go more noteworthy distances to find appropriate hunting grounds, prompting expanded energy use and decreased conceptive achievement.

Because of these difficulties, polar bears have shown a few conduct transformations, like investing more energy in land and rummaging for elective food sources. Notwithstanding, the drawn out endurance of polar bears is intently attached to tending to the main drivers of environmental change and relieving its effects on their living spaces.

Protection and Versatile Administration

Considering the natural difficulties looked by numerous species, preservation endeavors assume a basic part in protecting biodiversity and advancing the versatility of biological systems. Versatile administration, a methodology that perceives the powerful idea of biological systems and the requirement for adaptable techniques, is turning out to be progressively significant in protection rehearses.

Model: Coral Reef Protection

Coral reefs, among the most different biological systems on earth, face dangers like climbing ocean temperatures, coral dying, and sea fermentation. Preservation endeavors for coral reefs frequently include a blend of procedures, including marine safeguarded regions, rebuilding projects, and worldwide drives to diminish fossil fuel byproducts.

Versatile administration in coral reef preservation recognizes the intricacy of these biological systems and the vulnerability encompassing future circumstances. Observing and changing protection techniques because of new data and changing conditions are vital for guaranteeing the drawn out practicality of coral reef environments.

Mechanical Advancements as Natural Variations

In the cutting edge period, innovation plays had a huge impact in aiding life forms, including people, adjust to their surroundings. Mechanical advancements have given apparatuses and answers for address ecological difficulties and upgrade the versatility of both regular and human frameworks.

Model: Accuracy Horticulture

Accuracy horticulture is an illustration of how innovation is helping natural transformation in the domain of food creation. Using satellite symbolism, sensors, and information investigation, ranchers can upgrade the utilization of assets like water, composts, and pesticides. This expands the productivity of agrarian practices as well as limits the natural effect of cultivating, adding to economical food creation.

The Job of Training and Mindfulness in Natural Variation

Schooling and mindfulness are critical parts of encouraging ecological variation, both at the individual and cultural levels. Grasping the interconnectedness of biological systems, the effects of human exercises, and the significance of protection is fundamental for informed direction and mindful natural stewardship.

Model: Natural Training Projects

Natural training programs, whether in schools, networks, or through media, assume an essential part in bringing issues to light about ecological issues. These projects can engage people to pursue supportable decisions in their day to day routines, advocate for protection strategies, and add to an aggregate work to address natural difficulties.

4.1 Tolerance to Temperature Variations

Resilience to temperature varieties is a key part of the versatility of living organic entities to their surroundings. The capacity to endure and flourish in a scope of temperatures is pivotal for the endurance, development, and propagation of assorted species across various biological systems. From tiny microbes to complex multicellular organic entities, the instruments and methodologies utilized to endure temperature varieties are different and intriguing.

Microbial Resistance

Microorganisms, including microscopic organisms, archaea, and parasites, are probably the strongest life structures on The planet. They occupy a great many conditions, from the super cold of polar districts to the searing intensity of aqueous vents. One wonderful element of microbial life is its capacity to endure outrageous temperature varieties.

Model: Thermophiles and Psychrophiles

Thermophiles are microorganisms that flourish in high-temperature conditions, frequently surpassing the resistance furthest reaches of most other living things. These extremophiles can be found in geothermally warmed districts, for example, underground aquifers and remote ocean aqueous vents. They have adjusted to catalysts and cell structures that stay steady and practical at high temperatures.

On the opposite finish of the range, psychrophiles are adjusted to very cool conditions, for example, polar districts and remote ocean channels. These microorganisms have advanced instruments to keep up with cell capabilities at low temperatures, including the creation of radiator fluid proteins that forestall the arrangement of ice precious stones inside cells.

Plant Transformations to Temperature Varieties

Plants, as sessile life forms, display different variations to adapt to temperature changes. Their capacity to adapt to various temperature conditions is fundamental for fruitful germination, development, and multiplication.

Model: Cold Acclimation in Winter Wheat

Winter wheat (Triticum aestivum) gives a magnificent illustration of a plant's capacity to endure cold temperatures through a cycle known as chilly acclimation. As winter draws near, these plants go through physiological and biochemical changes that improve their cool resilience. This incorporates the collection of viable solutes, for example, sugars and proline, which go about as cryoprotectants, forestalling ice precious stone arrangement inside plant cells.

Moreover, changes in film lipid arrangement and the development of explicit proteins add to keeping up with cell layer honesty and capability at low temperatures. These transformations permit winter wheat and other cold-open minded plants to get by and proceed with development during cold weather months.

Creature Warm Guideline

Creatures, especially those with complex physiological frameworks, have developed different instruments to manage their internal heat level inside a reach that upholds ideal capability. The capacity to endure temperature varieties is significant for creatures' endurance, as it impacts metabolic cycles, chemical action, and in general physiological capability.

Model: Ectothermy and Endothermy

Creatures can be extensively characterized into ectothermic and endothermic classifications in view of their warm guideline procedures. Ectothermic creatures, like reptiles and creatures of land and water, depend on outside wellsprings of intensity to manage their internal heat level. They are in many cases more open minded toward temperature varieties, as their inside processes are not as firmly connected to a particular temperature range.

Endothermic creatures, including birds and vertebrates, keep a moderately steady inner internal heat level through metabolic intensity creation. This takes into consideration more noteworthy physiological action and versatility to different ecological circumstances. Notwithstanding, endothermic creatures might in any case display social transformations, like looking for shade or warmth, to adapt to outrageous temperatures.

Amphibian Transformations

Sea-going conditions present special moves for temperature resilience because of the distinctions in heat conductivity and warm security contrasted with air. Oceanic organic entities, the two plants, and creatures, have advanced explicit transformations to explore these difficulties.

Model: Warm Definition in Lakes

Lakes frequently show warm separation, where unmistakable layers of water have various temperatures. The epilimnion, or upper layer, is hotter and more oxygen-rich, while the hypolimnion, or lower layer, is colder and may have lower oxygen levels. Fish and other amphibian creatures might move upward through these layers to track down the ideal temperature for their metabolic necessities.

A few types of fish, like trout, are cold-water species and are adjusted to flourish in colder, very much oxygenated waters. Interestingly, warm-water fish, similar to dupe, have variations that permit them to endure higher temperatures. Understanding warm delineation is urgent for the preservation and the board of oceanic biological systems, as temperature varieties can impact the appropriation and conduct of sea-going organic entities.

Human Transformations to Temperature Varieties

Individuals, as an exceptionally versatile animal varieties, have created different social, conduct, and physiological techniques to adapt to temperature varieties. From apparel and sanctuary to cutting edge warming and cooling advancements, people have essentially extended their natural surroundings range by changing their surroundings and concocting devices to alleviate the effect of outrageous temperatures.

Model: Social Transformations to Cold Conditions

In chilly environments, human populaces have created explicit social transformations to adapt to low temperatures. Conventional apparel, for example, fur-lined pieces of clothing and protected boots, gives viable warm protection. Inuit people group, for instance, have shrewdly planned dress from creature skins that trap air, making a protecting layer to hold body heat.

Besides, conventional residences, similar to the igloo, grandstand structural transformations to keep up with warmth. These designs use the protecting properties of snow and ice, really giving a livable climate in frigid temperatures.

Environmental Change and Temperature Resilience Difficulties

While living organic entities have shown amazing flexibility to temperature varieties all through transformative history, the fast speed of contemporary environmental change presents uncommon difficulties. Worldwide temperature increments, changed precipitation examples, and outrageous climate occasions are influencing environments and species around the world.

Model: Coral Blanching

Coral reefs, profoundly delicate to temperature changes, are encountering the impeding impacts of environmental change. Raised ocean temperatures can instigate coral fading, a peculiarity where corals remove their harmonious green growth, prompting a deficiency of variety and nourishing assets. Assuming the pressure endures, corals might bite the dust.

This represents a critical danger to the biodiversity and biological elements of coral reefs, influencing marine environments that rely upon these different living spaces. Preservation endeavors are fundamental to alleviate the effects of environmental change on temperature-delicate biological systems and advance the versatility of weak species.

Mechanical Developments for Temperature Guideline

In the cutting edge period, innovation plays had a vital impact in improving temperature capacity to bear different purposes, from protecting food to establishing open to living and work spaces. Developments in warming, ventilation, and cooling (air conditioning) frameworks, as well as progressions in warm protection materials, add to temperature guideline in different settings.

Model: Environment Controlled Farming

Nursery innovation addresses a creative way to deal with temperature guideline in horticulture. By controlling temperature, stickiness, and other ecological elements, nurseries give an ideal developing climate to plants, broadening the developing season and expanding crop yields. This innovation is especially important in districts with outrageous temperatures or restricted arable land.

4.2 Salinity and pH Preferences

Saltiness and pH are basic natural factors that significantly impact the conveyance, conduct, and physiological cycles of living life forms. Whether in earthly, sea-going, or even extremophilic conditions, creatures have created unpredictable transformations to flourish inside unambiguous scopes of saltiness and pH. This extensive investigation dives into the meaning of saltiness and pH, the components living beings utilize to keep up with homeostasis, and the natural ramifications of deviations from ideal circumstances.

Grasping Saltiness

Definition and Estimation

Saltiness alludes to the centralization of broken up salts in water and is normally communicated as parts per thousand (ppt) or reasonable saltiness units (psu). The saltiness of regular waters can shift fundamentally, with freshwater conditions normally having low saltiness, while seawater is described by high saltiness.

Significance of Saltiness for Sea-going Creatures

Saltiness is a urgent component impacting the osmotic equilibrium of oceanic organic entities. Osmotic equilibrium is the harmony between the inside and outer centralizations of solutes, guaranteeing water development across cell layers without compromising cell honesty. Marine living beings, like fish and spineless creatures, have adjusted to higher outside salinities, while freshwater species keep up with transformations to bring down saltiness conditions.

Osmoregulation Components

Marine Osmoregulation

Marine living beings face the test of forestalling water misfortune in a high-saltiness climate. Fish, for instance, discharge overabundance salts through specific chloride cells in their gills and effectively take in water to keep up with inside osmotic equilibrium.

Freshwater Osmoregulation

On the other hand, freshwater life forms should forestall the convergence of water and effectively take-up salts to balance the weakening impacts of their current circumstance. This frequently includes the discharge of enormous volumes of weaken pee and the take-up of particles from the encompassing water.

Halophytes: Plants Adjusted to Saltiness

In earthly environments, halophytes are plants adjusted to flourish in saline soils. These plants have developed components to bar or endure high salt focuses. A few halophytes, similar to mangroves, effectively discharge salt through specific salt organs, while others, for example, succulents, store overabundance salts in vacuoles to forestall poisonousness.

Human Effect on Saltiness

Human exercises, especially agribusiness and industry, can modify saltiness levels in amphibian environments. Inordinate utilization of manures and the release of salt water from desalination plants can raise saltiness, influencing the piece of oceanic networks and presenting difficulties for freshwater organic entities.

Looking at pH Inclinations

Definition and Estimation

pH is a proportion of the corrosiveness or alkalinity of, not entirely settled by the centralization of hydrogen particles. The pH scale goes from 0 to 14, with values under 7 thought about acidic, 7 unbiased, or more 7 antacid.

Meaning of pH in Organic Frameworks

pH assumes a critical part in natural frameworks, impacting compound action, metabolic cycles, and the dissolvability of particles. Creatures show explicit pH inclinations, and deviations from their ideal pH reach can prompt physiological pressure or even demise.

Acidophiles and Alkaliphiles

Some extremophilic microorganisms, known as acidophiles and alkaliphiles, flourish in outrageous pH conditions. Acidophiles thrive in acidic circumstances, like acidic mine waste, while alkaliphiles possess soluble conditions, similar to soft drink lakes. These microorganisms have developed biochemical transformations to keep up with cell capability in conditions outside the common pH range for most living beings.

Amphibian pH Elements

Amphibian biological systems are especially delicate to changes in pH, with numerous oceanic organic entities showing explicit pH inclinations. Freshwater biological systems, for example, ordinarily have an unbiased to somewhat acidic pH, while marine conditions will generally be more soluble.

Corrosive Downpour and pH Adjustments

Human exercises, including the consuming of petroleum products, can add to the arrival of sulfur and nitrogen oxides into the climate. These mixtures can prompt the arrangement of corrosive downpour, which, when stored into sea-going environments, brings down pH levels. Fermentation of water bodies can unfavorably affect oceanic life, especially on species with tight pH resilience ranges.

Collaborations and Communications among Saltiness and pH

Estuarine Conditions

Estuarine conditions, where freshwater from waterways meets and blends in with seawater, exhibit the unique exchange among saltiness and pH. Creatures in estuaries should explore changes in both saltiness and pH, making a special natural setting that upholds different and versatile networks.

Carbonate Buffering Framework

The carbonate buffering framework is a key component impacting the pH of sea-going conditions. In seawater, carbonate particles go about as a cradle, assisting with keeping a generally steady pH notwithstanding contributions of acids or bases. The harmony between disintegrated carbon dioxide, bicarbonate particles, and carbonate particles is urgent for the general dependability of the marine climate.

Sea Fermentation

Human-actuated expansions in climatic carbon dioxide levels, basically from the consuming of petroleum products, have prompted elevated carbon dioxide retention by the world's seas. This outcomes in a diminishing in pH, a peculiarity known as sea fermentation. Sea fermentation presents huge difficulties for marine creatures, especially those with calcium carbonate skeletons or shells, like corals, mollusks, and certain planktonic organic entities.

Saltiness and pH Slopes in Oceanic Biological systems

In sea-going biological systems, saltiness and pH angles frequently coincide, affecting the dissemination of creatures along ecological changes. For instance, mangrove environments show inclinations from freshwater to marine circumstances, impacting the arrangement of plant and creature networks.

Contextual analyses in Saltiness and pH Transformations

Extraordinary Salt Lake, USA

The Incomparable Salt Lake in Utah, USA, is a limit hypersaline climate with saltiness levels a few times higher than that of the sea. The lake upholds remarkable microbial networks, including halophiles adjusted to the difficult circumstances. The collaboration between outrageous saltiness and pH makes a particular biological system with creatures adjusted to flourish in both high salt focuses and basic pH.

Mono Lake, USA

Mono Lake in California, USA, is one more eminent illustration of outrageous pH conditions. The lake has high alkalinity because of the presence of carbonate salts. Alkaliphilic microbes and different microorganisms have adjusted to thrive in this antacid climate, exhibiting the versatility of life to outrageous pH conditions.

The Dead Ocean

The Dead Ocean, situated at the absolute bottom on Earth's surface, is a hypersaline lake with saltiness levels that surpass those of most seas. The outrageous saltiness, combined with the high mineral substance, establishes a difficult climate for most sea-going life. Be that as it may, certain halophilic microorganisms and archaea have adjusted to flourish in the outrageous states of the Dead Ocean.

Human Effects and The executives Methodologies

Desalination Advancements

Desalination, the most common way of eliminating salts from seawater to deliver freshwater, is an undeniably used innovation to address water shortage in bone-dry areas. Nonetheless, the release of gathered salt water once again into normal water bodies presents difficulties to nearby environments, as it can change saltiness levels and effect marine life. Feasible desalination rehearses and the mindful administration of saline solution removal are essential contemplations in alleviating natural effects.

Maintainable Agribusiness Practices

Rural exercises can add to saltiness and pH changes in soils and water bodies. Embracing manageable horticultural practices, like accuracy water system and the utilization of salt-lenient harvests, can assist with limiting the effect on soil saltiness. Also, soil changes and legitimate supplement the board can support keeping up with ideal pH levels for crop development.

Moderating Sea Fermentation

Tending to the underlying drivers of sea fermentation, fundamentally lessening carbon dioxide discharges, is principal for the drawn out wellbeing of marine biological systems. Preservation endeavors, like the foundation of marine safeguarded regions and the improvement of versatile types of marine creatures, add to alleviating the effects of changing saltiness and pH conditions.

Future Points of view and Exploration Bearings

As environmental change speeds up and human exercises keep on forming the climate, understanding the communications among saltiness and pH turns out to be progressively essential. Future examination ought to zero in on disentangling the atomic components behind variations to outrageous circumstances, anticipating the biological results of adjustments in saltiness and pH, and creating imaginative advances for economical asset the board.

4.3 Responses to Environmental Stressors

Living life forms continually connect with their surroundings, experiencing different stressors that can affect their endurance and prosperity. Ecological stressors envelop an expansive scope of variables, remembering changes for temperature, saltiness, pH, toxins, environment misfortune, and that's just the beginning. Because of these stressors, organic entities have advanced a variety of versatile instruments to adapt to and moderate the impacts. This far reaching investigation digs into the assorted reactions to natural stressors across various degrees of organic association, from sub-atomic and physiological transformations to social and biological methodologies.

Sub-atomic and Cell Reactions

Stress-Responsive Qualities and Proteins

At the sub-atomic level, creatures have a collection of stress-responsive qualities and proteins that empower them to see and answer ecological difficulties. These sub-atomic reactions frequently include the actuation of flagging pathways that manage quality articulation. Heat shock proteins, for instance, are a class of sub-atomic chaperones that assist with safeguarding cells from harm brought about by raised temperatures. These proteins are blended in light of intensity stress and help with keeping up with legitimate protein collapsing and cell capability.

DNA Fix Components

Openness to ecological stressors, like radiation or contaminations, can harm DNA. Living beings have developed complex DNA fix components to correct these harms and keep up with genomic trustworthiness. DNA fix chemicals distinguish and address different sorts of DNA injuries, forestalling the gathering of transformations that could think twice about capability or lead to illnesses like disease.

Cancer prevention agent Guard Frameworks

Oxidative pressure, coming about because of a lopsidedness between the creation of receptive oxygen species (ROS) and the capacity of cells to detoxify them, is a typical outcome of ecological stressors. Life forms send cancer prevention agent guard frameworks to kill ROS and shield cells from oxidative harm. Catalysts like superoxide dismutase and catalase make light of critical jobs in breaking hurtful ROS and keeping up with cell redox balance.

Physiological Variations

Thermoregulation in Endotherms and Ectotherms

Temperature changes address a critical ecological stressor, and life forms have developed different physiological variations to manage their internal heat levels. Endothermic creatures, like vertebrates and birds, have the capacity to produce inward intensity through metabolic cycles, empowering them to keep a somewhat consistent internal heat level regardless of outer circumstances. Conversely, ectothermic creatures, including reptiles and creatures of land and water, depend on outer intensity sources to direct their internal heat level.

Osmoregulation in Amphibian Conditions

Amphibian life forms face difficulties connected with osmotic guideline, especially in conditions with fluctuating saltiness. Fish, for instance, utilize osmoregulatory instruments to keep up with the harmony between particles and water across their gills and body surfaces. Anadromous fish, similar to salmon, show transformations that permit them to change among freshwater and saltwater conditions during various phases of their life cycle.

Drying up Resilience in Xerophytes

Plants in parched conditions, known as xerophytes, have created transformations to adapt to water shortage and high temperatures. Succulents, for example, prickly plants, store water in particular tissues, permitting them to endure broadened times of dry spell. Also, xerophytes frequently have altered leaf structures, for example, diminished leaf surface region or the presence of trichomes, to limit water misfortune through happening.

Conduct Reactions

Relocation and Dispersal

Relocation is a boundless conduct transformation saw in light of changing ecological circumstances. Numerous types of birds, fish, and vertebrates embrace occasional movements to get to assets like food, rearing destinations, or reasonable environments. Dispersal, the development of people from their origination, is another conduct system that assists populaces with colonizing new territories and answer ecological changes.

Diapause and Lethargy

Bugs and different spineless creatures frequently enter diapause, a condition of suspended improvement, because of unfriendly natural circumstances. Diapause permits these creatures to endure troublesome seasons or times of shortage. Essentially, lethargy in plants includes a transitory discontinuance of development and metabolic action, empowering them to endure conditions like outrageous temperatures or water shortage.

Cover looking for Conduct

Despite ecological stressors, creatures might display cover looking for conduct to track down asylum from unfavorable circumstances. Desert creatures, for example, look for conceal during the most smoking pieces of the day to abstain from overheating. Tunneling creatures, similar to rodents, make underground safe houses to get away from outrageous temperatures and hunters.

Biological Reactions

Phenotypic Pliancy

Phenotypic pliancy alludes to the capacity of a living being to display various aggregates because of ecological prompts. This versatility permits living beings to streamline their qualities for explicit circumstances. Plants, for instance, can adjust their development designs, leaf morphology, and conceptive systems because of varieties in light, temperature, and supplement accessibility.

Local area Elements and Species Communications

Natural stressors can impact the elements of biological networks by modifying species piece, overflow, and communications. Rivalry for restricted assets might escalate, prompting shifts in local area structure. Moreover, mutualistic connections might be upset, influencing the advantageous collaborations between species. Understanding these biological reactions is urgent for anticipating the effects of ecological stressors on biodiversity and environment working.

Progression in Upset Living spaces

Unsettling influences, whether regular occasions like fierce blazes or human-prompted exercises like logging, can prompt environmental progression — the interaction by which an upset territory is colonized and bit by bit supplanted by a more intricate local area. Trailblazer species, frequently described by high conceptive rates and flexibility to unforgiving circumstances, start the colonization, preparing for the foundation of additional particular species as the environment goes through recuperation.

Anthropogenic Stressors and Preservation Difficulties

Contamination and Poison Openness

Human exercises, like modern cycles, agribusiness, and urbanization, add to different types of contamination. Openness to poisons and poisons presents critical difficulties to creatures, prompting physiological pressure, hereditary transformations, and populace declines. Endeavors to relieve contamination incorporate the execution of natural guidelines, manageable practices, and the improvement of innovations for contamination control.

Living space Obliteration and Fracture

Living space obliteration and fracture, frequently determined by metropolitan turn of events and land-use changes, upset regular environments and effect biodiversity. Divided environments can confine populaces, diminish hereditary variety, and hinder relocation designs. Preservation procedures mean to address these difficulties through the foundation of safeguarded regions, living space rebuilding drives, and practical land-use arranging.

Environmental Change and A dangerous atmospheric devation

Environmental change, driven by human-initiated factors, for example, ozone depleting substance discharges, represents a multi-layered challenge for biological systems and organic entities around the world. Increasing temperatures, changing precipitation examples, and ocean level ascent can adjust territories and upset species conveyances. Preservation endeavors should address these difficulties by advancing environment versatile biological systems, lessening fossil fuel byproducts, and working with the transformation of weak species.

Preservation Methodologies and Versatile Administration

Safeguarded Regions and Biodiversity Preservation
The foundation of safeguarded regions, including public parks, natural life stores, and marine safe-havens, assumes an essential part in rationing biodiversity and giving places of refuge to weak species. These regions assist with relieving the effects of territory annihilation and give open doors to environmental reclamation and examination.

Rebuilding Nature
Rebuilding nature centers around the restoration of corrupted biological systems through the renewed introduction of local species, environment recreation, and the expulsion of obtrusive species. Rebuilding projects plan to improve biological system strength, advance biodiversity, and reproduce useful biological systems that can endure natural stressors.

Reasonable Asset The board
Reasonable asset the board rehearses are fundamental for offsetting human necessities with natural preservation. Practices like maintainable ranger service, fisheries the executives, and horticultural methodologies that focus on soil wellbeing and biodiversity add to the drawn out soundness of environments and decrease the effect of stressors on regular assets.

Versatile Administration Approaches
Versatile administration includes an adaptable and iterative way to deal with protection, recognizing the vulnerability and intricacy of environmental frameworks. By persistently gaining from the executives activities, adjusting methodologies in view of new data, and including partners in direction, versatile administration improves the viability of protection endeavors despite dynamic ecological stressors.

Chapter 5

Bioluminescence And Communication

Bioluminescence, the creation and emanation of light by living life forms, is an enrapturing and far and wide peculiarity in the regular world. This ability to interest has developed autonomously across different taxa, including microbes, parasites, bugs, fish, and, surprisingly, a few earthbound vertebrates. Past its tasteful allure, bioluminescence serves critical environmental capabilities, especially in the domain of correspondence. This investigation dives into the entrancing universe of bioluminescence, unwinding its components, natural jobs, and the complicated manners by which creatures use light creation for correspondence.

Figuring out Bioluminescence

The Atomic Component

Bioluminescence is fundamentally determined by the enzymatic response between luciferin, a light-discharging color, and oxygen, worked with by the protein luciferase. The cycle includes the oxidation of luciferin within the sight of oxygen, bringing about the arrival of photons, or light. Various creatures utilize varieties of this fundamental instrument, with some having extra proteins that upgrade or adjust the light-producing process.

Ordered Variety

Bioluminescence isn't bound to a particular scientific classification; it has freely developed in a wide exhibit of creatures. Models incorporate bioluminescent microscopic organisms like Vibrio fischeri, which structures advantageous associations with specific marine creatures; parasites like Mycena and Armillaria; and different marine spineless creatures, including jellyfish, squids, and shellfish.

Transformations for Disguise

In specific marine organic entities, bioluminescence fills in as a type of counter-enlightenment cover. This variation includes the creation of light to match the power and shade of the surrounding light, successfully delivering the organic entity imperceptible to hunters and prey looking upwards. Some remote ocean animals, like the lanternfish, use this technique to hide themselves from hunters prowling underneath.

The Environmental Jobs of Bioluminescence
Ruthless Procedures

Bioluminescence frequently assumes a pivotal part in the predation procedures of specific creatures. Hunters can utilize bioluminescent baits to draw in prey in obscurity profundities of the sea. The anglerfish, for example, has a bioluminescent draw hanging before its mouth, which it uses to draw in more modest fish in the completely dark pit, making them clueless prey.

Safeguard Systems

Bioluminescence can likewise work as a safeguard system. A few creatures discharge bioluminescent mists or blazes while undermined, confounding or surprising their hunters. The ink cloud radiated by a few bioluminescent squids, for instance, fills in as a diversionary strategy, permitting the squid to escape from hunters while they are immediately diverted.

Regenerative Flagging

Bioluminescence frequently assumes a significant part in conceptive flagging, permitting creatures to draw in mates and convey during romance ceremonies. Fireflies, for example, utilize synchronized glimmering examples to flag their accessibility and draw in likely mates. The coordination of these blazes is urgent for fruitful mating, and people that can keep up with the beat really increment their possibilities tracking down a reasonable accomplice.

Correspondence in Friendly Organic entities

In specific species, bioluminescence works with correspondence inside gatherings. Frontier creatures like specific jellyfish show composed bioluminescent presentations, empowering correspondence between people inside the province. The synchronization of light emanation is remembered to improve bunch union, deflect hunters, and possibly draw in prey.

Bioluminescence in Earthbound Conditions

While bioluminescence is frequently connected with marine organic entities, it likewise happens in earthly conditions. Fireflies, which have a place with the Lampyridae family, are maybe the most notable illustration of bioluminescent living beings ashore. Fireflies use their bioluminescence for romance, with guys transmitting explicit glimmering examples to draw in females. This captivating presentation of light is an exemplary illustration of bioluminescence's job in correspondence inside earthly environments.

Bioluminescence and Human Association
Logical Exploration and Medication

Bioluminescence has critical applications in logical examination and medication. The compound luciferase, got from bioluminescent living beings, is broadly utilized in biotechnology as a journalist quality. Its capacity to create light permits researchers to follow quality articulation, concentrate on cell processes, and imagine natural peculiarities. Furthermore, the firefly luciferase framework has been utilized in clinical diagnostics, where it fills in as a touchy marker for different tests.

The travel industry and Feel

Bioluminescent showcases, especially those including dinoflagellates or certain jelly-fish, have become attractions in ecotourism. Areas with bioluminescent inlets, where the water gleams with the development of living beings, draw guests looking for a hypnotizing regular exhibition. The tasteful allure of bioluminescence has likewise motivated specialists and movie producers, who frequently integrate this charming peculiarity into their works.

Natural Checking

Bioluminescent living beings, especially microscopic organisms, are utilized in eco-logical checking to distinguish the presence of explicit impurities. Bioassays in light of bioluminescence are proficient devices for surveying water quality, recognizing toxins, and checking natural wellbeing. The awareness of bioluminescent creatures to changes in their environmental elements makes them significant marks of natural pressure.

Dangers to Bioluminescent Creatures

Regardless of the biological importance and enthralling nature of bioluminescence, numerous living beings that display this quality face dangers from human exercises and ecological changes. Contamination, natural surroundings obliteration, and environ-mental change can upset the sensitive equilibrium of biological systems, influencing the dispersion and overflow of bioluminescent living beings. Light contamination, brought about by fake lighting, represents a specific danger to animal groups that depend on bioluminescence for correspondence and cover, as it can disrupt their normal ways of behaving.

Protection Endeavors and Future Exploration

Protection endeavors pointed toward safeguarding bioluminescent organic entities include the conservation of their living spaces, diminishing contamination, and bring-ing issues to light about the environmental significance of these organic entities. Laying out marine safeguarded regions, limiting light contamination, and advancing reasonable the travel industry rehearses are basic moves toward defending the living spaces of bioluminescent species.

Future exploration in bioluminescence envelops many roads. Figuring out the atomic components fundamental bioluminescence in various living beings, investi-gating the natural jobs of bioluminescence in assorted conditions, and exploring the possible uses of bioluminescent proteins in biotechnology are regions that keep on charming researchers. Propels in imaging advances and hereditary control procedures give new apparatuses to disentangling the secrets of bioluminescence and its more extensive ramifications for science and biology.

5.1 The Significance of Bioluminescence in Jellyfish

Jellyfish, having a place with the phylum Cnidaria, are marine spineless creatures known for their coagulated bodies and elegant developments. Among the different dazzling elements showed by jellyfish, bioluminescence stands apart as one of the most fascinating and huge. Bioluminescence, the capacity of living organic entities to create light, assumes an essential part in the science, nature, and, surprisingly, possible utilizations of jellyfish. This investigation dives into the meaning of bioluminescence in jellyfish, disentangling the components behind this peculiarity, its natural jobs, and the arising applications in exploration and innovation.

Figuring out Bioluminescence in Jellyfish

System of Bioluminescence

The bioluminescence showed by jellyfish is principally worked with by the collaboration between a light-discharging particle called luciferin, the compound luciferase, and oxygen. The response among luciferin and oxygen, catalyzed by luciferase, brings about the discharge of light. On account of jellyfish, the light is regularly blue or green, making an entrancing showcase when seen in obscurity waters.

Aequorin and Green Fluorescent Protein (GFP)

Jellyfish, especially species like Aequorea victoria, have been instrumental in the disclosure and comprehension of bioluminescence. Aequorin, a photoprotein viewed as in A. victoria, is answerable for the underlying blue light emanation. The ensuing green light discharge, regularly alluded to as green fluorescent protein (GFP), is a consequence of the change of a blue light middle.

The revelation and ensuing detachment of GFP have altered sub-atomic and cell science. GFP can be hereditarily designed and combined to different proteins, permitting scientists to imagine and follow explicit cell processes in living creatures, including human cells. This forward leap, for which the pioneers were granted the Nobel Prize in Science in 2008, has had significant ramifications for biomedical exploration and the comprehension of cell elements.

Biological Jobs of Bioluminescence in Jellyfish

Predation and Protection

Bioluminescence in jellyfish fills various biological needs, with predation and safeguard being among the most noticeable. A jellyfish use their bioluminescent capacity to draw in prey. In the remote ocean climate, where daylight is scant, jellyfish can utilize their bioluminescence to bait little life forms towards their limbs, supporting prey catch.

On the other hand, bioluminescence can likewise act as a protective instrument. When compromised by hunters, certain jellyfish discharge bioluminescent glimmers, making an interruption or frightening impact. This protective presentation might befuddle or prevent hunters, giving the jellyfish a chance to get away.

Correspondence and Generation

Bioluminescence assumes a critical part in correspondence and propagation among jellyfish. During the mating season, some jellyfish species participate in perplexing romance customs including bioluminescent showcases. The coordination of light discharge designs is believed to be a way for people to perceive reasonable mates and take part in effective proliferation.

Furthermore, bioluminescence can support intraspecific correspondence inside a populace of jellyfish. Facilitated presentations of light discharge can upgrade bunch union, possibly assisting jellyfish with exploring in dim waters or direction aggregate developments.

Cover and Counter-Enlightenment

For specific remote ocean jellyfish, bioluminescence is a device for cover and counter-light. Counter-enlightenment includes the discharge of light to match the encompassing light circumstances, actually making the jellyfish less apparent to hunters or prey looking upwards. This variation permits jellyfish to mix into the general climate and stay away from recognition in obscurity profundities of the sea.

Remarkable Bioluminescent Jellyfish Species

Aequorea victoria

Aequorea victoria, regularly known as the precious stone jellyfish or the green fluorescent protein jellyfish, is a little, straightforward jellyfish saw as in the Pacific Northwest. It acquired noticeable quality in logical exploration because of the disclosure of aequorin and green fluorescent protein (GFP) in its tissues. The bioluminescence of A. victoria plays had a urgent impact in progressing sub-atomic and cell science, especially in the field of fluorescence microscopy.

Cypridinid Jellyfish

A few types of jellyfish having a place with the Cypridinidae family are known for their remarkable bioluminescent showcases. These jellyfish produce eruptions of light, making stunning special visualizations. The cadenced and synchronized blazes of light are remembered to fill needs like correspondence, hunter prevention, or prey fascination. Cypridinid jellyfish are usually tracked down in remote ocean conditions.

Turritopsis dohrnii

The Turritopsis dohrnii, frequently alluded to as the "eternal jellyfish," is known for its capacity to return its cells to a previous stage and restart its life cycle. While not especially bioluminescent, this jellyfish species has stood out for its surprising regenerative capacities. Research on T. dohrnii may have suggestions for figuring out maturing and regenerative medication.

Bioluminescence Applications and Innovative Bits of knowledge

Bioluminescent Proteins in Exploration

The disclosure and detachment of bioluminescent proteins, especially GFP, have groundbreakingly affected natural exploration. GFP and its variations are generally utilized as atomic markers, permitting researchers to follow and picture explicit proteins or cell structures inside living organic entities. This progressive device has applications in assorted fields, including cell science, hereditary qualities, neuroscience, and medication.

Bioluminescence Imaging

Bioluminescence imaging (BLI) is a painless imaging method that uses the light transmitted by bioluminescent creatures or cells to picture natural cycles in living subjects. In research, this strategy is regularly utilized in examinations including quality articulation, cell following, and the observing of illness movement. BLI has applications in both preclinical exploration and clinical diagnostics.

Ecological Observing

Bioluminescent organic entities, including specific jellyfish species, have been utilized in ecological observing and poisonousness testing. Bioassays in light of bioluminescence give a delicate and quick method for surveying the presence of pollutants in water bodies. The responsiveness of bioluminescent life forms to changes in their current circumstance makes them significant marks of natural wellbeing.

Bioluminescent Workmanship and Plan

The captivating sparkle of bioluminescence has roused craftsmen, fashioners, and draftsmen. Integrating bioluminescent components into workmanship establishments, style, and, surprisingly, building plans has turned into an inventive undertaking. The tasteful allure of bioluminescence can possibly consolidate science and craftsmanship, cultivating a more profound appreciation for the miracles of the normal world.

Difficulties and Protection Contemplations

Dangers to Bioluminescent Jellyfish

Jellyfish populaces, incorporating those with bioluminescent capacities, face different dangers in the present evolving climate. Human-prompted factors, for example, environmental change, contamination, overfishing, and natural surroundings corruption can affect jellyfish populaces and their biological systems. These stressors might influence the overflow and circulation of bioluminescent jellyfish species.

Light Contamination

Light contamination, brought about by the exorbitant and misled utilization of counterfeit light, represents a particular danger to bioluminescent living beings. In marine conditions, fake light can slow down regular ways of behaving like hunter evasion, prey fascination, and correspondence. Moderating light contamination is fundamental for saving the biological jobs of bioluminescence in jellyfish and other marine organic entities.

Preservation Systems

Preservation endeavors for bioluminescent jellyfish include tending to more extensive marine protection challenges. Safeguarding marine environments, carrying out supportable fishing practices, and diminishing contamination are critical stages in guaranteeing the strength of jellyfish populaces. Furthermore, bringing issues to light about the environmental significance of bioluminescent creatures can add to public help for protection drives.

Future Headings and Logical Investigation

Genomic Bits of knowledge

Progresses in genomics and atomic science have empowered researchers to dig further into the hereditary premise of bioluminescence in jellyfish. Concentrating on the genomes of bioluminescent species can give experiences into the advancement and variety of the qualities answerable for light creation. Similar genomics might uncover the hereditary variations that underlie the different natural jobs of bioluminescence in jellyfish.

Biotechnological Applications

The novel properties of bioluminescent proteins, particularly GFP, keep on moving biotechnological advancements. Designed variations of GFP are being produced for different applications, including biosensors, imaging specialists, and remedial devices. The adaptability of bioluminescent proteins opens up additional opportunities for their utilization in clinical diagnostics, drug disclosure, and natural checking.

Remote ocean Investigation

Numerous bioluminescent jellyfish species possess the profundities of the sea, where natural circumstances are outrageous and less investigated. Progressions in remote ocean investigation advancements, like remotely worked vehicles (ROVs) and independent submerged vehicles (AUVs), empower researchers to concentrate on bioluminescent creatures in their normal environments. Revelations in the remote ocean might uncover new species and shed light on the transformations of jellyfish to these difficult conditions.

5.2 Communication within Jellyfish Populations

Jellyfish, having a place with the phylum Cnidaria, are entrancing marine organic entities known for their coagulated bodies, limbs, and novel methods of development. While generally viewed as basic spineless creatures, ongoing examination has uncovered complex ways of behaving and correspondence systems inside jellyfish populaces. This complete investigation digs into the complicated universe of correspondence inside jellyfish networks, revealing insight into the different instruments, flagging modalities, and biological ramifications of their connections.

Life systems and Conduct of Jellyfish

Fundamental Life systems

Jellyfish display a basic body structure, portrayed by a thick chime or umbrella-formed body, limbs outfitted with stinging cells called nematocysts, and a focal mouth situated on the underside of the ringer. While coming up short on an incorporated sensory system, jellyfish have a diffuse nerve net that organizes their fundamental engine capabilities.

Development and Velocity

Jellyfish utilize a beating development to explore through the water. By contracting and loosening up their ringer molded bodies, they produce water flows that impel them forward. This musical throb is a major part of their velocity and is fundamental for catching prey, staying away from hunters, and taking part in regenerative ways of behaving.

Compound Flagging

Pheromones and Compound Correspondence

Compound flagging assumes an essential part in the correspondence methodologies of numerous marine creatures, and jellyfish are no special case. Jellyfish discharge synthetic mixtures, frequently as pheromones, into the water to pass data on to conspecifics. These substance prompts can fill different needs, including drawing in mates, demonstrating the presence of food, or flagging alert because of hunters.

Mating Pheromones

During the mating season, a few types of jellyfish discharge explicit pheromones to draw in expected mates. The acknowledgment of these substance signals is fundamental for fruitful generation, as it permits people to find and coordinate with reasonable mates. The interchange of compound flagging and conduct reactions during jellyfish romance customs is a captivating part of their conceptive systems.

Alert Pheromones

Jellyfish can deliver alert pheromones in light of seen dangers. At the point when a jellyfish is gone after or harmed, it might deliver synthetic signs into the water, making close by conspecifics aware of the likely risk. This type of synthetic correspondence helps coordinate cautious reactions inside the populace, permitting people to make an equivocal move or embrace protective stances.

Visual Correspondence

Bioluminescence as a Visual Sign

Bioluminescence, the capacity of creatures to deliver light, is a wonderful type of visual correspondence among jellyfish. While certain species use bioluminescence for hunting or deflecting hunters, others utilize it for of intraspecific correspondence. The planned blazing of bioluminescent signs inside a populace is remembered to pass data related on to mating, hunter evasion, or gathering union.

Romance Showcases

In specific jellyfish species, visual correspondence through bioluminescent showcases is vital to romance customs. Male and female jellyfish might take part in unpredictable light shows, organizing their bioluminescent examples as a feature of the romance cycle. The synchronization of these presentations is urgent for effective mating, featuring the job of obvious prompts in regenerative ways of behaving.

Bunch Coordination

Visual correspondence is likewise fundamental for planning bunch developments inside jellyfish populaces. Certain species show synchronized swimming examples, with people changing their beating developments and bioluminescent presentations because of conspecifics. This aggregate conduct upgrades bunch attachment and may serve different capabilities, including hunter discouragement and route.

Mechanical Flagging

Contact and Mechanical Awareness

While jellyfish need complex tactile organs, they are equipped for identifying mechanical improvements through specific designs. Contact receptors, situated on their appendages and chime, permit jellyfish to detect actual contact with their current circumstance and conspecifics. This material responsiveness assumes a part in different ways of behaving, including prey catch, route, and reactions to ecological prompts.

Accumulation and Amassing

Mechanical flagging adds to the arrangement of jellyfish conglomerations or multitudes. People inside a populace can detect the developments and throbs of neighboring conspecifics, prompting the aggregate conduct saw in swarms. Totals of jellyfish fill various needs, for example, upgrading taking care of productivity, giving assurance from hunters, and working with conceptive exercises.

Hear-able Correspondence

Sound Creation in Jellyfish

While customarily not related with sound creation, ongoing investigations have proposed that some jellyfish species might be equipped for delivering low-recurrence sounds. The specific components and motivations behind sound creation in jellyfish are still being scrutinized, however this arising part of their correspondence collection opens new roads for research.

Estimated Capabilities

The elements of sound creation in jellyfish stay speculative, however speculations remember its job for correspondence, route, and possibly hindering hunters. The capacity to deliver sounds could offer extra ways for jellyfish to trade data inside their populaces, particularly in conditions where visual or compound flagging might be restricted.

Natural Effects on Correspondence

Temperature and Natural Variables

The adequacy of correspondence inside jellyfish populaces is affected by different ecological variables. Temperature, saltiness, and other water quality boundaries can influence the transmission of compound signs, influencing the reach and adequacy of correspondence. Understanding the natural requirements on jellyfish correspondence is fundamental for appreciating their ways of behaving and populace elements.

Light Circumstances

In sufficiently bright conditions, visual correspondence through bioluminescence might be more articulated, impacting the ways of behaving of jellyfish populaces. Conversely, in hazier or more profound waters, where visual signs might be less successful, compound and mechanical correspondence become more essential. The exchange between various methods of correspondence permits jellyfish to adjust to fluctuating light circumstances in their living spaces.

Social Association and Collective vibes

Total and Multitude Conduct

Jellyfish are known for their aggregative ways of behaving, shaping gatherings or multitudes that display facilitated developments. These accumulations might fluctuate in size and design, with people beating and swimming in synchrony. The arrangement of multitudes fills different needs, including further developed searching effectiveness, insurance against hunters, and expanded conceptive achievement.

Size and Arrangement

The size and arrangement of jellyfish totals can shift broadly among species. Some structure huge, thick multitudes, while others might accumulate in more modest gatherings. The arrangement of these conglomerations might incorporate people of various sizes and formative stages. Understanding the variables that impact the size and piece of jellyfish bunches is basic for unwinding the complexities of their social association.

Social Ordered progressions

Perceptions recommend the presence of social orders inside jellyfish populaces. Certain people might display positions of authority, affecting the developments and ways of behaving of others inside the gathering. The components hidden the foundation of social pecking orders and the elements that decide influential positions are areas of progressing research.

Conceptive Correspondence

Mating Customs and Romance

Regenerative correspondence is a pivotal part of jellyfish ways of behaving, working with mate acknowledgment and fruitful mating. Mating customs frequently include complicated romance presentations, where people coordinate their developments and bioluminescent signs. The synchronization of these showcases is fundamental for guaranteeing that viable mates perceive one another and participate in fruitful regenerative exercises.

Arrival of Gametes

The arrival of gametes, either eggs or sperm, is a planned interaction inside jellyfish populaces. Ecological prompts, like changes in temperature, light circumstances, or substance signals, may set off the synchronous arrival of gametes by various people. This simultaneous gamete discharge improves the possibilities of fruitful preparation and adds to the regenerative progress of the populace.

Hunter Prey Collaborations

Hunting and Prey Catch

Jellyfish are entrepreneurial hunters that feed on various little creatures, including microscopic fish, fish hatchlings, and, surprisingly, other jellyfish. Correspondence assumes a part in hunting and prey catch, where jellyfish utilize a mix of visual, compound, and mechanical signs to distinguish and seek after likely prey. The coordination of these signs improves their proficiency in finding and catching prey in their amphibian surroundings.

Guard Components

Correspondence inside jellyfish populaces is likewise fundamental for protection against hunters. When compromised, jellyfish can deliver caution signals, including substance prompts and bioluminescent blazes, to alarm close by conspecifics. The planned reactions of the populace, like changes in swimming examples or the arrival of bodily fluid, may help deflect or befuddle hunters and upgrade the aggregate guard of the gathering.

Correspondence in Various Jellyfish Species

Species-Explicit Correspondence

Correspondence systems can fluctuate fundamentally among various jellyfish species. While certain species depend vigorously on visual presentations and bioluminescence, others might focus on substance flagging or mechanical signs. The variety of correspondence components mirrors the variations of jellyfish to their particular surroundings, natural specialties, and life chronicles.

Remote ocean Jellyfish

Jellyfish occupying remote ocean conditions face one of a kind difficulties, including low light circumstances and outrageous tensions. Remote ocean jellyfish have developed specific variations in their correspondence methodologies, possibly depending more on synthetic flagging or sound creation. Understanding the correspondence elements of remote ocean jellyfish gives experiences into the variations of marine life to outrageous conditions.

Biological Ramifications

Populace Elements

Correspondence inside jellyfish populaces has significant ramifications for their biological elements. The coordination of ways of behaving, like collection, amassing, and conceptive exercises, impacts populace size, appropriation, and flexibility. Changes in ecological circumstances, human exercises, or regular occasions can affect the correspondence examples of jellyfish populaces, prompting shifts in their natural jobs.

Trophic Collaborations

Jellyfish are essential parts of marine food networks, impacting trophic communications and supplement cycling. Correspondence inside jellyfish populaces influences their collaborations with different living beings, including prey things, hunters, and contenders. Understanding the trophic jobs of jellyfish and their correspondence intervened consequences for environment elements is significant for marine biology and preservation.

Blossom Development

Under specific circumstances, jellyfish populaces can go through quick expansions in overflow, prompting the development of blossoms. The variables impacting sprout development, including correspondence elements, are complicated and multi-layered. Blossoms can have flowing consequences for marine biological systems, influencing fisheries, supplement cycling, and the design of tiny fish networks.

Human Collaboration and Protection

Human Effect on Jellyfish Correspondence

Human exercises, for example, overfishing, contamination, and environmental change, can impact the correspondence elements of jellyfish populaces. Changes in water quality, territory debasement, and modifications in prey accessibility might disturb the normal ways of behaving and correspondence examples of jellyfish. Understanding the connections between human exercises and jellyfish correspondence is essential for creating powerful protection systems.

Protection Difficulties

Jellyfish populaces face preservation challenges, including environment misfortune, overfishing, and the effects of environmental change. Preservation endeavors should think about the natural jobs of jellyfish, their correspondence elements, and the possible outcomes of human-actuated aggravations. Carrying out manageable fisheries works on, moderating contamination, and safeguarding marine natural surroundings are fundamental parts of jellyfish preservation.

Biological system Flexibility

The strength of marine environments to jellyfish blossoms and their natural effects is a subject of continuous examination. While jellyfish assume significant parts in marine food networks and supplement cycling, their excess can prompt disturbances in biological system balance. Concentrating on the correspondence elements of jellyfish populaces adds to how we might interpret how biological systems answer ecological changes and human exercises.

Future Exploration Bearings

Propels in Innovation

Mechanical headways, including submerged mechanical technology, hereditary devices, and high level imaging procedures, offer new roads for concentrating on jellyfish correspondence. Remote detecting advancements, like independent submerged vehicles (AUVs) and remotely worked vehicles (ROVs), empower specialists to notice jellyfish ways of behaving in their regular natural surroundings, giving significant experiences into their correspondence elements.

Atomic and Hereditary Examinations

Progresses in sub-atomic and hereditary examinations permit researchers to investigate the sub-atomic premise of correspondence inside jellyfish populaces. Inspecting the qualities related with tactile insight, signal transduction, and reaction to natural prompts gives a more profound comprehension of the components basic jellyfish ways of behaving. Similar genomics across various jellyfish species offers experiences into the advancement of correspondence methodologies.

Environmental Change and Natural Effects

Research on the effects of environmental change on jellyfish correspondence is turning out to be progressively significant. Changes in sea temperature, corrosiveness, and flows can impact the dissemination and ways of behaving of jellyfish populaces. Concentrating on how jellyfish answer environment prompted modifications in their surroundings adds to how we might interpret marine biological system elements in an impacting world.

Interdisciplinary Methodologies

The investigation of jellyfish correspondence benefits from interdisciplinary methodologies that incorporate science, environment, physical science, and designing. Joint efforts between scientists, oceanographers, physicists, and specialists can yield exhaustive bits of knowledge into the instruments, capabilities, and natural ramifications of jellyfish correspondence. This interdisciplinary methodology upgrades our capacity to resolve complex inquiries regarding jellyfish ways of behaving and their job in marine environments.

5.3 Role in Predator Avoidance and Mating Rituals

Bioluminescence, the capacity to deliver light, is an enthralling and far reaching peculiarity in the regular world. Among marine organic entities, jellyfish stand apart for their mind boggling utilization of bioluminescence, utilizing it for both hunter aversion and mating customs. This investigation dives into the double job of bioluminescence in jellyfish, disentangling the components behind these ways of behaving, the biological importance, and the complex transaction between methods for surviving and conceptive achievement.

Bioluminescence in Jellyfish: An Outline

Prior to digging into the particular jobs of bioluminescence in jellyfish ways of behaving, it's fundamental to comprehend the central systems driving this enrapturing peculiarity. Bioluminescence in jellyfish includes the enzymatic response between a light-producing particle called luciferin, the chemical luciferase, and oxygen. The oxidation of luciferin within the sight of oxygen brings about the discharge of light, commonly in the blue or green range. Jellyfish utilize this interaction to create glimmers, gleams, or composed light shows, and the job of bioluminescence reaches out past simple enlightenment.

Hunter Evasion Techniques

Disguise and Counter-Brightening

One of the essential jobs of bioluminescence in jellyfish is hunter evasion through the components of disguise and counter-brightening. In the immense profundities of the sea, where daylight lessens, predation turns into a difficult errand. Here, jellyfish influence their bioluminescence to mix into their environmental factors or control the light climate.

Cover:

Some jellyfish species use bioluminescence for cover by emanating strike that matches the encompassing light circumstances. This transformation makes them less apparent to hunters or prey looking upwards, successfully camouflaging them against the foundation. The procedure includes a type of mimicry, where the jellyfish changes its bioluminescence to match the force and shade of the light separating down from the surface.

Counter-Brightening:

Counter-brightening is one more hunter evasion methodology utilized by specific jellyfish. Rather than matching the encompassing light, these jellyfish emanate light ventrally to check the outline made by their bodies against the foundation light. This makes them less obvious to hunters prowling underneath, really decreasing the gamble of being recognized and gone after.

Frightening Hunters: Bioluminescent Blazes

Notwithstanding cover, some jellyfish utilize bioluminescent glimmers as a surprising instrument against hunters. At the point when undermined or gone after, these jellyfish discharge unexpected eruptions of light, making a diverting and confusing impact on the hunter. This protective way of behaving can alarm and befuddle the aggressor, furnishing the jellyfish with a chance to get away.

Mating Ceremonies: Bioluminescence in Conceptive Ways of behaving

While bioluminescence is a urgent device for hunter evasion, it likewise assumes an essential part in the conceptive ways of behaving of jellyfish. Mating ceremonies include perplexing showcases of light, planned developments, and explicit examples of bioluminescence that work with mate acknowledgment and fruitful proliferation.

Romance Presentations

Jellyfish take part in romance presentations during the mating season, a period set apart by unambiguous ecological prompts. The romance ceremonies are intricate, including the organized utilization of bioluminescence to flag availability to mate and draw in reasonable accomplices. These showcases are species-explicit, with every jellyfish species having unmistakable examples and arrangements of light emanations.

Synchronization of Bioluminescent Examples:

In numerous jellyfish species, romance showcases are described by the synchronization of bioluminescent examples. Male and female jellyfish coordinate their glimmers or sparkles, making an outwardly dazzling and synchronized dance. The capacity to keep up with this coordination is vital for effective mating, guaranteeing that viable mates perceive one another and take part in the regenerative cycle.

Flagging Conceptive Wellness:

Bioluminescence in romance showcases fills in as a flagging system for regenerative wellness. The power, recurrence, and coordination of light emanations can pass on data about the wellbeing and life of the people in question. Mates might utilize these signs to survey the nature of likely accomplices, adding to the general progress of the mating system.

Gamete Delivery: Synchronized Bioluminescence

The arrival of gametes, a critical occasion in jellyfish generation, is in many cases joined by synchronized bioluminescence inside the populace. Ecological prompts, like changes in temperature, light circumstances, or synthetic signs, trigger the synchronous arrival of eggs and sperm by different people. This synchronized gamete discharge upgrades the possibilities of fruitful treatment and adds to the regenerative progress of the populace.

Interchange between Hunter Evasion and Mating Ceremonies
Compromises and Transformative Techniques

The double job of bioluminescence in hunter evasion and mating ceremonies addresses an entrancing transformative compromise. On one hand, the capacity to stay away from hunters through disguise and counter-enlightenment improves the endurance chances of jellyfish in their normal territories. Then again, the utilization of bioluminescence in mating ceremonies is fundamental for conceptive achievement, guaranteeing the continuation of the species.

Ecological Triggers

The ecological triggers for these ways of behaving are unpredictably connected. The accessibility of assets, natural circumstances, and the presence of potential mates are factors that impact when and how jellyfish utilize bioluminescence. Understanding the exchange between hunter aversion and mating ways of behaving reveals insight into the versatile methodologies that have developed in jellyfish populaces over the long haul.

Occasional and Circadian Rhythms

The planning of hunter aversion and mating ways of behaving frequently follows occasional and circadian rhythms. Ecological signs, like changes in temperature or light accessibility, can set off unambiguous ways of behaving. The synchronized arrival of gametes or the inception of romance presentations might be impacted by these cadenced examples, guaranteeing that regenerative occasions are very much planned for ideal achievement.

Job of Chemicals and Compound Flagging

Chemicals and compound flagging probably assume a critical part in organizing both hunter evasion and mating ways of behaving in jellyfish. Ecological boosts can set off the arrival of explicit chemicals, impacting the declaration of bioluminescent proteins and the inception of ways of behaving. The reconciliation of hormonal motioning with other natural signs adds to the coordinated reactions saw in jellyfish populaces.

Natural Importance and Protection Suggestions
Trophic Connections and Biological system Elements

The double job of bioluminescence in hunter aversion and mating customs has significant ramifications for trophic cooperations and environment elements. Jellyfish, as the two hunters and prey, possess a pivotal situation in marine food networks. Their ways of behaving impact the overflow and dispersion of prey things, shape hunter prey connections, and add to supplement cycling in marine biological systems.

Blossom Arrangement and Populace Elements

Understanding the natural meaning of bioluminescence in jellyfish ways of behaving is especially significant with regards to sprout development. Jellyfish blossoms, described by quick expansions in populace overflow, can have flowing consequences for marine environments. The exchange between hunter evasion and mating ways of behaving impacts populace elements, and changes in natural circumstances can affect the recurrence and force of jellyfish sprouts.

Preservation Contemplations

The preservation of jellyfish populaces requires a thorough comprehension of their ways of behaving, remembering the job of bioluminescence for hunter evasion and mating customs. Human-actuated factors, for example, overfishing, contamination, and environmental change, can disturb these ways of behaving and lead to shifts in jellyfish populaces. Preservation techniques should think about the environmental jobs of jellyfish and their commitments to marine biological system wellbeing.

Future Exploration Bearings
Sub-atomic and Hereditary Bits of knowledge

Progressions in sub-atomic and hereditary examinations offer energizing roads for unwinding the complexities of bioluminescence in jellyfish. Investigating the qualities related with the development of bioluminescent proteins, the guideline of light outflow, and the mix of tangible data gives a sub-atomic comprehension of these ways of behaving. Relative genomics across various jellyfish species can uncover the developmental transformations that have formed bioluminescence in different genealogies.

Mechanical Developments

Mechanical developments, including submerged mechanical technology, high level imaging procedures, and ecological sensors, improve our capacity to concentrate on jellyfish ways of behaving in their regular natural surroundings. Remote detecting advances, like independent submerged vehicles (AUVs) and remotely worked vehicles (ROVs), empower scientists to notice bioluminescent presentations, hunter aversion systems, and mating ceremonies in exceptional detail.

Environmental Change and Ecological Effects

Research on the effects of environmental change on jellyfish ways of behaving is a basic area of examination. Changes in sea temperature, causticity, and flows can impact the dispersion and exercises of jellyfish populaces. Understanding what these natural changes mean for bioluminescence, hunter evasion, and mating ways of behaving gives experiences into the versatile limits of jellyfish despite worldwide ecological movements.

Interdisciplinary Methodologies

The investigation of bioluminescence in jellyfish benefits from interdisciplinary co-ordinated efforts that incorporate science, nature, hereditary qualities, and innovation. Joint efforts between specialists from different fields improve how we might interpret the perplexing communications between hunter aversion and mating ways of behaving. Coordinating environmental information with sub-atomic bits of knowledge and innovative perceptions adds to a comprehensive comprehension of jellyfish science.

Chapter 6

Interactions with Other Species

Jellyfish, with their entrancing yet mysterious presence, assume complex parts in marine environments through communications with a different exhibit of animal groups. From predation and rivalry to advantageous connections and natural impacts, the communications of jellyfish with different organic entities shape the elements of the seas. This investigation dives into the many-sided snare of connections that jellyfish lay out with various species, revealing insight into the biological importance and transformative variations that portray these collaborations.

Predation and the Job of Jellyfish as Hunters

Jellyfish as Artful Hunters

Jellyfish display crafty taking care of ways of behaving, going after various little life forms inside their span. Their appendages, outfitted with specific stinging cells called nematocysts, are utilized for catching prey. Normal prey things incorporate little fish, fish hatchlings, tiny fish, and, surprisingly, other jellyfish. The ruthless idea of jellyfish positions them as critical players in marine food networks, impacting the overflow and dissemination of prey species.

Influence on Fish Populaces

In specific biological systems, jellyfish predation can have flowing consequences for fish populaces. For instance, when jellyfish go after fish hatchlings, they can impact enlistment levels and the general design of fish networks. The interaction between jellyfish predation and fish elements is intricate and fluctuates across various marine conditions.

Trophic Fountains and Biological system Elements

The predation effect of jellyfish is important for bigger trophic fountains that echo through marine environments. Changes in jellyfish overflow can impact the populaces of their prey, influencing the whole food web. Trophic fountains started by jellyfish have been seen in regions where their populaces go through quick builds, prompting shifts in local area construction and elements.

Rivalry for Assets

Asset Rivalry with Fish and Tiny fish

Jellyfish frequently contend with fish and tiny fish for shared assets, like zooplankton and little fish. The opposition is impacted by factors like prey accessibility, ecological circumstances, and the regenerative systems of both jellyfish and their rivals. Understanding these asset elements is essential for anticipating what changes in jellyfish overflow might mean for other marine species.

Overfishing and Jellyfish Blossoms

Human exercises, especially overfishing, can adjust the equilibrium of marine environments and add to the multiplication of jellyfish. At the point when fish populaces decline due to overfishing, it can make a vacuum in the biological system that jellyfish are appropriate to take advantage of. This peculiarity has been seen in regions where overfishing has prompted expanded jellyfish blossoms, further underscoring the multifaceted connection among jellyfish and fish populaces.

Advantageous Connections

Advantageous interaction with Adolescent Fish

While jellyfish are frequently seen as hunters, a few animal categories take part in co-operative associations with adolescent fish. Adolescent fish look for shelter among the limbs of specific jellyfish species, acquiring assurance from predation. Consequently, the jellyfish benefit from the presence of the fish, which might give security against possible hunters and add to the jellyfish's general wellness.

Harmonious Relationship with Microorganisms

Jellyfish likewise structure advantageous relationship with microorganisms, including microbes and green growth. These connections add to the wholesome necessities of the jellyfish and may assume a part in their general wellbeing. The mind boggling cooperations among jellyfish and microorganisms feature the interconnectedness of marine life and the significance of advantageous connections in supplement cycling.

Natural Impacts

Effect of Natural Circumstances

Jellyfish communications with different species are fundamentally impacted by ecological circumstances, including temperature, saltiness, and supplement accessibility. Changes in these variables can influence the dissemination and overflow of jellyfish, impacting their connections with the two contenders and prey. Understanding the natural triggers for jellyfish ways of behaving is essential for foreseeing their biological effect in an evolving environment.

Environmental Change and Jellyfish Elements

The worldwide peculiarity of environmental change acquaints extra intricacies with jellyfish associations. Warming seas, adjusted flows, and changes in supplement accessibility can impact the dissemination examples of jellyfish species. A few examinations recommend that jellyfish populaces might flourish in hotter waters, possibly prompting expanded communications with different species and affecting marine environments.

Medusivores: Particular Hunters of Jellyfish

Ocean Anemones and Nudibranchs

Certain species have advanced particular variations to benefit from jellyfish, procuring them the name of "medusivores." Ocean anemones and nudibranchs are among the life forms that have created remarkable instruments to catch and consume jellyfish. These communications add to the perplexing equilibrium inside marine biological systems and embody the variety of taking care of procedures that have advanced because of the commonness of jellyfish.

Sunfish and Leatherback Turtles

Enormous marine life forms, like sea sunfish (mola) and leatherback turtles (Dermochelys coriacea), are known to benefit from jellyfish. These species have variations that permit them to proficiently consume jellyfish. The cooperations between these marine goliaths and jellyfish show the more extensive environmental jobs that jellyfish play in supporting different trophic levels.

Exploring Jellyfish Sprouts

Influence on Fisheries

Jellyfish sprouts, portrayed by fast expansions in jellyfish overflow, can altogether affect fisheries. Sprouts might obstruct fishing exercises by harming gear, stopping up nets, and lessening get quality. The financial ramifications of jellyfish sprouts highlight the requirement for successful administration techniques to relieve their effect on fisheries.

Versatile Techniques of Fish

Some fish species have created versatile techniques to explore conditions with high jellyfish overflow. For instance, certain fish display ways of behaving, for example, swimming in designs that limit contact with jellyfish limbs. Understanding the co-evolutionary elements among fish and jellyfish adds as far as anyone is concerned of how species adjust to changing environmental circumstances.

Human-Jellyfish Associations

Fisheries and Monetary Effects

The cooperations among jellyfish and human exercises reach out past natural elements to incorporate financial and cultural effects. In locales where jellyfish sprouts upset fisheries, the monetary outcomes can be significant. Techniques to relieve these effects include creating advancements to keep jellyfish from impeding fishing stuff and tracking down elective purposes for reaped jellyfish.

The travel industry and Public Mindfulness

Jellyfish cooperations with people additionally happen with regards to the travel industry and diversion. A few types of jellyfish have stinging cells that can make distress or injury people. Public mindfulness crusades, wellbeing measures, and exploration on jellyfish ways of behaving add to limiting the dangers related with human-jellyfish cooperations in seaside regions.

Developmental Variations

Advancement of Stinging Cells

The nematocysts, or stinging cells, found in jellyfish limbs are exceptional developmental variations that assume a focal part in their collaborations with different species. These particular cells empower jellyfish to catch prey, prevent hunters, and guard against contenders. The variety of nematocyst types mirrors the transformative systems that have arisen in light of various environmental difficulties.

Transformative Reactions to Ecological Changes

Jellyfish display developmental pliancy, permitting them to answer ecological changes over the long haul. As marine conditions go through shifts because of regular cycles or human-instigated factors, jellyfish populaces might develop to adjust to new circumstances. Understanding the transformative reactions of jellyfish upgrades our capacity to anticipate their associations with different species notwithstanding continuous ecological changes.

Preservation Suggestions

Adjusting Hunter and Prey Elements

Endeavors to save marine biological systems should consider the fragile harmony among hunter and prey elements including jellyfish. Overfishing, contamination, and environmental change can disturb this equilibrium, prompting shifts in jellyfish overflow and collaborations with different species. Feasible fisheries the executives and marine protection methodologies are fundamental for keeping up with the environmental honesty of marine biological systems.

Overseeing Jellyfish Blossoms

Tending to the financial and natural effects of jellyfish sprouts requires compelling administration systems. Observing natural circumstances, understanding the triggers for jellyfish sprouts, and creating advancements to forestall or relieve their consequences for fisheries are significant parts of effective jellyfish blossom the board.

Public Mindfulness and Instruction

Advancing public mindfulness and instruction about jellyfish collaborations is vital to limiting contentions with human exercises. Illuminating beach front networks, anglers, and travelers about jellyfish ways of behaving, wellbeing measures, and the biological jobs of jellyfish adds to an agreeable conjunction among people and these marine life forms.

Future Exploration Headings

Atomic Bits of knowledge into Collaborations

Propels in sub-atomic science offer energizing roads for acquiring further bits of knowledge into the atomic premise of jellyfish cooperations. Investigating the qualities related with nematocyst improvement, the creation of bioluminescent proteins, and the sub-atomic reactions to ecological changes gives a nuanced comprehension of the systems driving jellyfish ways of behaving.

Environmental Change and Natural Versatility

Research on the effects of environmental change on jellyfish cooperations and natural versatility is an advancing field. Researching how jellyfish populaces answer warming seas, adjusted flows, and changing supplement accessibility adds to how we might interpret the versatile limits of marine biological systems despite worldwide ecological difficulties.

Coordinated Ways to deal with Marine Administration

The intricacy of jellyfish associations requires coordinated ways to deal with marine administration. Coordinated efforts between researchers, policymakers, and partners are fundamental for creating thorough procedures that consider the biological, monetary, and cultural elements of jellyfish elements. Coordinated administration approaches add to the manageability of marine biological systems and the prosperity of seaside networks.

6.1 Symbiotic Relationships with Fish and Invertebrates

The huge domains of the sea harbor an orchestra of harmonious connections, and among the hypnotizing artists in this submerged expressive dance are jellyfish. These coagulated animals, frequently saw as singular strays, participate in multifaceted organizations with an assortment of fish and spineless creatures. This investigation digs into the entrancing universe of advantageous connections among jellyfish and their amphibian colleagues, disentangling the complexities of mutualistic, commensal, and parasitic associations that portray these submerged collusions.

Mutualistic Advantageous interaction: Giving Asylum and Acquiring Insurance

Jellyfish and Adolescent Fish: A Defensive Partnership

One of the most enrapturing instances of mutualistic advantageous interaction including jellyfish is their relationship with adolescent fish. Certain fish species look for shelter among the limbs of jellyfish, tracking down safe-haven from hunters and using the jellyfish's defensive umbrella as a safeguard. Consequently, jellyfish benefit from this course of action by acquiring assurance from expected hunters for their adolescent fish colleagues.

Components of Security:

The defensive job of jellyfish for adolescent fish includes numerous systems. The limbs of jellyfish, furnished with stinging cells called nematocysts, go about as an obstruction to numerous hunters. The complicated dance of the jellyfish limbs gives a unique obstruction that prevents expected dangers, offering a place of refuge for the more modest fish to explore the territories of the vast sea.

Species-Explicit Affiliations:

The relationship among jellyfish and adolescent fish are in many cases species-explicit, with specific fish favoring explicit jellyfish species for shelter. The mutualistic bond is definitely not an irregular event however a finely tuned transformation that has developed over the long run, featuring the explicitness and intricacy of these submerged organizations.

Shielding Among the Arms: Commensalism in the Pit

Notwithstanding adolescent fish looking for shelter, other more modest organic entities, like scavangers and minuscule spineless creatures, may take on a commensal relationship with jellyfish. Commensalism is a kind of beneficial interaction where one animal groups benefits, and the other is neither fundamentally hurt nor made a difference. The limbs of jellyfish, following through the water, make a moving microhabitat that more modest living beings can use for safe house and transport.

Catching a ride on Jellyfish:

A few little spineless creatures and shellfish participate in a novel type of commensalism by catching a ride on the thick collections of jellyfish. These small travelers explore the sea flows by getting a ride on the drifting jellyfish, accessing new taking care of grounds and potential open doors for endurance without forcing a massive expense on their jellyfish has.

The Dance of Light: Bioluminescent Advantageous interaction

Jellyfish and Bioluminescent Microorganisms: A Brilliant Organization

The sea profundities are enlightened by a supernatural dance of bioluminescent light, and in this captivating presentation, jellyfish and certain bioluminescent microorganisms participate in a cooperative relationship. Some jellyfish harbor bioluminescent microscopic organisms inside their tissues, making a striking sparkle that fills different natural needs.

Component of Bioluminescence:

The bioluminescent microbes, ordinarily having a place with the sort Vibrio, live in particular designs inside the jellyfish, like concentrated light organs. The cooperation between the jellyfish and these microscopic organisms brings about the emanation of light. This bioluminescent presentation isn't just enrapturing however serves significant natural capabilities for the two accomplices.

Natural Importance:

The bioluminescence in jellyfish is accepted to assume a part in hunter evasion, with the brilliant sparkle possibly preventing hunters or confounding them. Furthermore, the light transmitted by the jellyfish might draw in prey, adding to the general progress of the jellyfish as a hunter. This harmonious relationship exhibits the union of organic cycles for the common advantage of the two accomplices.

Parasitic Affiliations: Taking advantage of the Host

The Clouded Side of Beneficial interaction: Parasitism by Amphipods

While numerous cooperative connections are portrayed by shared advantage or lack of bias, a few affiliations include a parasitic accomplice that exploits its host. Certain types of amphipods, little shellfish, are known to participate in parasitic associations with jellyfish.

Amphipods as Parasites:

Amphipods might connect themselves to the thick tissue of jellyfish, benefiting from their host's body liquids. This parasitic affiliation can be hindering to the jellyfish, possibly influencing their wellbeing and regenerative achievement. The amphipods, in any case, benefit by acquiring food from the jellyfish without giving any clear advantage consequently.

Influence on Jellyfish:

The effect of amphipod parasitism on jellyfish changes among species. At times, the presence of amphipods might prompt decreased swimming capacities and compromised wellbeing in jellyfish. The parasitic relationship features the assorted results that advantageous affiliations can have on the wellness and endurance of the interfacing species.

Natural Effects on Advantageous Connections

Temperature, Supplements, and Cooperative Elements

The elements of cooperative connections among jellyfish and different species are fundamentally impacted by natural variables. Temperature, supplement accessibility, and other biological boundaries can influence the commonness and progress of these associations. Understanding the ecological effects on cooperative connections adds to our more extensive appreciation of the flexibility and strength of marine environments.

Environmental Change and Advantageous Associations:

As the worldwide environment goes through changes, including sea warming and modified supplement cycling, the elements of cooperative connections might be impacted. Changes in temperature can impact the circulation of species engaged with cooperative affiliations, possibly prompting changes in the predominance and progress of these organizations. The many-sided dance of beneficial interaction is subsequently complicatedly connected to the more extensive ecological setting.

Occasional Examples and Conceptive Techniques

The planning of advantageous connections frequently follows occasional examples, lining up with regenerative methodologies and ecological signs. Adolescent fish looking for asylum among jellyfish appendages might do as such during explicit periods when ecological circumstances are positive for both the jellyfish and the fish. The irregularity of harmonious associations adds one more layer of intricacy to the natural embroidery of marine biological systems.

Preservation Suggestions and Biological system Wellbeing

Adjusting Cooperative Connections for Biological system Strength

The fragile equilibrium of harmonious connections inside marine biological systems adds to the general wellbeing and solidness of these perplexing trap of life. Preservation endeavors should think about the effects of human exercises, for example, overfishing and contamination, on the elements of cooperative organizations. Guaranteeing the safeguarding of these connections is crucial for supporting the biodiversity and strength of marine environments.

Overfishing and Jellyfish-Fish Affiliations:

Overfishing can disturb the fragile equilibrium of harmonious connections including jellyfish and fish species. The expulsion of specific fish species through overfishing might prompt an irregularity in the elements of jellyfish-fish affiliations, impacting the dispersion and wealth of the two accomplices. Practical fisheries the executives is critical for keeping up with the soundness of these advantageous cooperations.

Biological system Administrations and Biodiversity

Harmonious connections add to the arrangement of biological system administrations, including supplement cycling, hunter prevention, and upgraded regenerative achievement. The variety of these collaborations improves the general biodiversity of marine environments, giving an abundance of biological administrations that help the working of the seas. Protection endeavors that focus on the safeguarding of advantageous connections add to the upkeep of biodiversity and biological system wellbeing.

Future Exploration Headings

Sub-atomic Experiences into Harmonious Instruments

Headways in sub-atomic science offer energizing roads for acquiring further experiences into the components driving advantageous connections among jellyfish and different species. Investigating the qualities related with cooperative affiliations, the sub-atomic flagging pathways included, and the reactions to ecological changes gives an atomic comprehension of the complexities of these submerged organizations.

Environmental Change and Cooperative Strength

Research on the effects of environmental change on cooperative connections is a basic area of examination. Understanding how climbing temperatures, changing supplement accessibility, and adjusted sea flows impact the elements of harmonious organizations adds as far as anyone is concerned of the versatile limits of marine life forms even with worldwide ecological movements.

Protection Techniques for Cooperative Collaborations

The protection of cooperative collaborations requires incorporated procedures that consider the biological, financial, and cultural components of marine environments. Coordinated efforts between researchers, policymakers, and partners are fundamental for creating complete protection designs that focus on the safeguarding of advantageous connections and the general soundness of marine environments.

6.2 Predators of Jellyfish and Defense Mechanisms

Jellyfish, with their ethereal elegance and spellbinding excellence, exist as the two hunters and prey in the tremendous scopes of the sea. While they use particular stinging cells called nematocysts to catch prey, they likewise explore the waters with a sharp consciousness of the various hunters that prowl in the profundities. This investigation digs into the many-sided dance between the hunters of jellyfish and the protection components these thick animals utilize to make due in the dynamic and serious marine climate.

Hunters of Jellyfish: A Different Cluster

Sea Sunfish (mola): The Delicate Goliath

The sea sunfish, or mola, addresses one of the biggest hard fish in the sea and is known for its impossible to miss appearance and giant size. Notwithstanding its size, the sea sunfish is a delicate goliath that takes care of fundamentally on jellyfish. This preference for jellyfish positions the sea sunfish as a central member in controlling jellyfish populaces and molding the elements of marine biological systems.

Taking care of Methodology:

The sea sunfish utilizes a remarkable taking care of system while consuming jellyfish. It moves toward the jellyfish in an upward direction, situating itself close to the thick mass. Utilizing its huge, adjusted body, the sea sunfish immerses the jellyfish in its mouth, where the delicate bodied structure considers simple ingestion. This taking care of conduct represents the versatility of specific marine species to gain by the bountiful assets given by jellyfish blossoms.

Leatherback Turtles (Dermochelys coriacea): Sea Pilots and Jellyfish Hunters

Leatherback turtles, famous for their huge size and unmistakable weathered shells, are imposing hunters on the planet's seas. Their eating regimen incorporates an assortment of jellyfish animal groups, and their utilization of these coagulated organic entities is a fundamental part of their searching way of behaving.

Particular Variations:

Leatherback turtles have developed specific transformations to work with jellyfish utilization. The design of their throat incorporates spines and in reverse pointing papillae, forestalling the break of elusive prey. This transformation permits leatherback turtles to proficiently catch and ingest jellyfish, highlighting the developmental weapons contest among hunters and their thick prey.

Ocean Anemones: Nematocyst-Safe Hunters

While ocean anemones are normally fixed hunters, they have fostered an interesting methodology for benefiting from jellyfish. A few types of ocean anemones are nematocyst-safe, meaning they are not impacted by the stinging cells of jellyfish. These ocean anemones can catch and consume jellyfish without setting off the nematocysts, exhibiting the variety of transformations in the weapons contest among hunters and their thick prey.

Component of Utilization:

Ocean anemones utilize their appendages to entrap the jellyfish, bringing it towards their focal mouth. The nematocyst obstruction permits the ocean anemones to control the jellyfish without setting off the cautious stinging cells. The inventiveness of this predation technique features the continuous developmental elements among jellyfish and their assorted arrangement of hunters.

Ocean Slugs and Nudibranchs: Variations for Consuming Jellyfish

Certain ocean slugs and nudibranchs have created astounding transformations for benefiting from jellyfish. These gastropods explore the difficulties acted by nematocysts like well as influence the poisons delivered by some jellyfish species for their own safeguard.

Integrating Nematocysts:

Some ocean slugs and nudibranchs are fit for integrating nematocysts from the jellyfish they consume into their own tissues. The nematocysts give these gastropods a protective instrument against expected hunters. This remarkable procedure of "natural burglary" grandstands the complex manners by which marine life forms adjust to take advantage of the highlights of their prey.

Fish Hunters: A Different Exhibit of Jellyfish Purchasers

Different fish species add to the predation on jellyfish, featuring the versatility of marine biological systems to oblige a different cluster of jellyfish shoppers. Models incorporate the sunfish (Lampris spp.), butterflyfish (Chaetodon spp.), and certain types of fish. The consideration of jellyfish in the weight control plans of these fish species mirrors the complicated collaborations inside marine food networks.

Scavenging Ways of behaving:

Fish hunters utilize different scavenging ways of behaving to catch jellyfish. Some utilization their mouths to overwhelm the jellyfish, while others might utilize attractions taking care of to catch individual appendages. The pervasiveness of jellyfish in the weight control plans of different fish species highlights the meaning of these coagulated living beings as a food source in marine biological systems.

Safeguard Instruments of Jellyfish: The Specialty of Endurance

Nematocysts: Stinging Cells as an Imposing Safeguard

At the core of the jellyfish's safeguard munititions stockpile lies the nematocyst — a specific stinging cell that infuses poisons into likely dangers. These minute weapons are conveyed along the limbs and group of jellyfish, filling in as an impressive hindrance against hunters.

System of Nematocyst Release:

At the point when set off by actual contact, nematocysts release with striking velocity, conveying poisons that immobilize or deflect expected dangers. The nematocyst reaction isn't just a critical part of jellyfish predation yet additionally an indispensable part of their safeguard against hunters. The intensity of the poisons changes among jellyfish species, affecting the adequacy of their guarded technique.

Bioluminescence: Enlightening a Cautious Showcase

Bioluminescence, the capacity of specific jellyfish species to deliver light, serves as a hypnotizing show as well as a protective instrument. Some jellyfish species use bioluminescence to make brilliant blazes or shows while undermined, frightening hunters and possibly stopping them.

Alarm Reaction:

The alarm reaction prompted by bioluminescence can be a compelling procedure for jellyfish to avoid predation. By making unexpected explosions of light, jellyfish muddle possible dangers, setting out a freedom for escape. The double job of bioluminescence in both hunter evasion and romance presentations features its diverse nature in the existence of jellyfish.

Straightforwardness and Cover: Mixing into the Blue

The clear and frequently straightforward nature of jellyfish fills in as a type of normal cover in the untamed sea. Jellyfish can mix into their environmental elements, making them less obvious to hunters and possibly improving their capacity to dodge recognition.

Counter-Enlightenment:

A few types of jellyfish utilize a type of counter-brightening, where they discharge strike that matches the encompassing light circumstances. This versatile system permits jellyfish to stay subtle by limiting their outline against the foundation. The capacity to mix into the blue breadth of the vast sea addresses a refined safeguard against visual hunters.

Coagulated Sythesis: A Dangerous Methodology

The coagulated sythesis of jellyfish isn't just urgent for their lightness yet in addition assumes a part in protection. The tricky and delicate bodied design of jellyfish can make them trying for hunters to get a handle on and consume.

Dangerous Departure:

At the point when faced by an expected danger, jellyfish can participate in an elusive getaway by getting their ringer and limbs. This constriction removes water, lessening their thickness and making them harder to hold. The coagulated surface, joined with the tricky break technique, adds to the general guard of jellyfish against actual predation.

Recovery: Flexibility Notwithstanding Predation

Jellyfish display wonderful regenerative abilities, permitting them to recuperate from predation endeavors and wounds. The capacity to recover harmed or cut off body parts, including arms, improves their versatility despite predation pressure.

Regrowth of Limbs:

After a predation occasion or injury, jellyfish can regrow their limbs, reestablishing their savage and guarded capacities. This regenerative capacity is a demonstration of the flexibility of jellyfish in adjusting to the difficulties presented by their dynamic marine climate.

Hunter Prey Elements: Difficult exercise in the Marine Environment

Trophic Communications: Molding Marine Food Networks

The predation on jellyfish and the protection components they convey add to the unpredictable embroidery of trophic cooperations inside marine biological systems. As jellyfish are devoured by various hunters, their populaces are controlled, forestalling unrestrained expansion and keeping an equilibrium in marine food networks.

Trophic Fountains:

The communications among jellyfish and their hunters can start trophic fountains, affecting the overflow and conveyance of different species inside the environment. For instance, the utilization of jellyfish by leatherback turtles might affect the conveyance of jellyfish species, accordingly impacting the overflow of their prey and the organic entities at lower trophic levels.

Effect of Human Exercises: Disturbing the Equilibrium

Human exercises, including overfishing and contamination, can disturb the sensitive equilibrium of hunter prey elements including jellyfish. Overfishing of jellyfish hunters, for example, leatherback turtles, can prompt a lopsidedness, permitting jellyfish populaces to flood. The results of this unevenness incorporate jellyfish blossoms that can influence fisheries, modify marine biological systems, and influence the general soundness of the seas.

Overfishing and Trophic Interruption:

The exhaustion of jellyfish hunters through overfishing makes a trophic disturbance that resounds through marine biological systems. Without regular controls on jelly-fish populaces, these coagulated creatures might multiply, impacting the overflow of their prey and adjusting the design of marine food networks. Supportable fisheries the executives is basic for keeping up with the equilibrium of hunter prey elements in the seas.

Environmental Change and Hunter Prey Cooperations

The worldwide peculiarity of environmental change acquaints extra intricacies with hunter prey cooperations including jellyfish. Changes in sea temperatures, flows, and supplement accessibility can impact the dissemination and ways of behaving of both jellyfish and their hunters.

Temperature Impacts:

As seas warm, the appropriation of jellyfish species might move, affecting the accessibility of these thick life forms as prey. Moreover, temperature changes can influence the ways of behaving and searching examples of jellyfish hunters, prompting shifts in hunter prey connections. Understanding the environment driven changes in hunter prey elements is urgent for anticipating the eventual fate of marine biological systems.

Human Points of view: Monetary Effects and The executives Methodologies

Influence on Fisheries: Financial Outcomes

The collaborations among jellyfish and their hunters have monetary ramifications, especially with regards to fisheries. Jellyfish blossoms can obstruct fishing exercises, harming gear, lessening get quality, and influencing the livelihoods of anglers.

Financial Expenses:

The financial expenses of jellyfish sprouts stretch out past direct obstruction with fishing activities. The exhaustion of fish populaces because of jellyfish predation can prompt decreased gets, influencing the monetary reasonability of fisheries. The financial results feature the requirement for viable administration systems to moderate the effect of jellyfish on fisheries.

The board Techniques: Moderating the Effect

To address the financial and biological effects of jellyfish predation, different administration systems have been proposed and carried out. These procedures expect to work out some kind of harmony between the protection of marine environments and the feasible utilization of fisheries assets.

Early Admonition Frameworks:

Carrying out early advance notice frameworks for jellyfish sprouts permits fisheries and seaside networks to plan for possible effects. Observing ecological circumstances, like water temperature and supplement levels, can give important experiences into the probability of jellyfish blossoms. Early identification empowers proactive measures to limit the monetary effect on fisheries.

Mechanical Developments:

Mechanical developments, including submerged mechanical technology and natural sensors, add to how we might interpret jellyfish elements. Remote detecting innovations, like independent submerged vehicles (AUVs) and remotely worked vehicles

(ROVs), take into consideration constant checking of jellyfish populaces and their cooperations with the marine climate.

Feasible Fisheries The executives:

Taking on supportable fisheries the board rehearses is fundamental for keeping up with the equilibrium of hunter prey elements in marine biological systems. This incorporates executing get limits, safeguarding basic territories, and tending to over-fishing of both jellyfish hunters and economically significant fish species. Economical administration adds to the flexibility and wellbeing of marine biological systems.

Future Exploration Bearings

Conduct Nature of Jellyfish: Unwinding Complex Associations

Headways in the field of conduct environment offer energizing roads for unwinding the mind boggling cooperations among jellyfish and their hunters. Concentrating on the ways of behaving of both jellyfish and their hunters in their normal natural surroundings gives bits of knowledge into the subtleties of hunter prey elements, including rummaging techniques, reaction systems, and the effect of ecological factors.

Atomic Experiences into Safeguard Instruments

Investigating the sub-atomic premise of jellyfish protection systems, especially the development of poisons and the activity of nematocysts, gives a more profound comprehension of the biochemical cycles included. Progresses in atomic science permit scientists to explore the qualities and sub-atomic pathways related with jellyfish guard, revealing insight into the developmental transformations that have molded these components.

Environmental Change and Hunter Prey Versatility

Research on the versatility of hunter prey collaborations even with environmental change is a basic area of examination. Understanding how shifts in sea temperatures, flows, and supplement accessibility impact the versatility of both jellyfish and their hunters adds as far as anyone is concerned of the biological effects of worldwide ecological changes.

Local area Environment of Jellyfish Blossoms

The people group environment of jellyfish blossoms includes analyzing the collaborations among jellyfish and different species inside the biological system. Concentrating on the local area elements during jellyfish sprouts gives bits of knowledge into the flowing impacts on marine food networks, supplement cycling, and the general design of the biological system. Coordinating people group nature points of view upgrades how we might interpret the more extensive environmental ramifications of jellyfish elements.

6.3 Impact on Ecosystems and Food Chains

Effect of Jellyfish on Biological systems and Established pecking orders: Disentangling the Gradually expanding influencesJellyfish, with their powerful magnificence and charming science, assume a multi-layered part in marine biological systems, applying both immediate and circuitous effects on the complex embroidery of life underneath the waves. This investigation dives into the effect of jellyfish on biological systems and pecking orders, disentangling the intricate elements that unfurl as these coagulated life forms explore the sea domains.

Environmental Meaning of Jellyfish

Cornerstone Species or Shrewd Sprouts?

Jellyfish are much of the time viewed as sharp species that can flourish under specific ecological circumstances, bringing about blossoms that catch the consideration of researchers, policymakers, and the public the same. While their populaces can flood because of elements like overfishing, environmental change, and supplement enhancement, the natural job of jellyfish is a subject of continuous discussion.

Cornerstone Species:

In specific biological systems, jellyfish are viewed as cornerstone species, assuming an essential part in forming the construction and capability of the local area. Their predation on zooplankton and little fish can impact the overflow of these prey species, making flowing impacts all through the food web. Understanding the nuanced associations among jellyfish and different parts of marine environments is fundamental for unwinding their biological importance.

The Trophic Place of Jellyfish

Jellyfish possess different trophic levels inside marine food networks, partaking both as hunters and prey. This complex job positions them as powerful supporters of the progression of energy and supplements inside environments.

Hunters of Zooplankton:

Certain jellyfish species feed on zooplankton, applying hierarchical control on these little creatures. By controlling zooplankton populaces, jellyfish impact the accessibility of assets for different species inside the food web, including little fish that depend on zooplankton as an essential food source.

Prey for Hunters:

At the same time, jellyfish act as prey for a different cluster of hunters, going from ocean turtles and fish to specific spineless creatures. The utilization of jellyfish by these hunters adds to the exchange of energy inside marine biological systems, forming the elements of trophic connections.

Jellyfish Sprouts: Causes and Outcomes

Ecological Triggers for Blossoms

Jellyfish sprouts, described by the fast and now and again overpowering multiplication of jellyfish populaces, can be set off by different natural variables. These variables remember changes for temperature, supplement accessibility, and adjustments in the wealth of contenders and hunters.

Environmental Change and Sea Warming:

The warming of seas because of environmental change is a critical component impacting jellyfish sprouts. Hotter temperatures can incline toward the regenerative achievement and development of jellyfish, prompting expanded blossom events in specific districts. The effect of environmental change on the recurrence and power of jellyfish sprouts highlights the interconnected idea of worldwide natural changes.

Supplement Enhancement:

Unreasonable supplement input into marine environments, frequently coming about because of human exercises, for example, horticulture and wastewater release, can add to jellyfish blossoms. Supplement improvement can upgrade the development of phytoplankton, an essential food hotspot for zooplankton. At the point when zooplankton populaces flood, jellyfish, as their hunters, may likewise encounter expanded overflow.

Overfishing and Trophic Disturbance:

The overfishing of specific fish species, especially those that go after jellyfish or vie for comparative assets, can make trophic uneven characters that favor jellyfish blossoms. Diminished predation tension on jellyfish and changed serious communications inside the biological system might add to the expansion of these thick life forms.

Results of Jellyfish Sprouts

Jellyfish blossoms can have sweeping ramifications for marine biological systems, affecting different parts of the food web and environment structure.

Rivalry with Fish:

During sprouts, jellyfish can rival fish for food assets, including zooplankton. The expanded predation on zooplankton by jellyfish might restrict the accessibility of this essential food hotspot for fish hatchlings and adolescents, possibly influencing fish populaces.

Predation on Fish Eggs and Hatchlings:

Some jellyfish species are known to benefit from fish eggs and hatchlings. The predation pressure applied by jellyfish on the early life phases of fish can impact the enlistment progress of fish populaces, with possible consequences for business fisheries.

Modified Energy Move:

The utilization of jellyfish by hunters rearranges energy inside marine environments. While specific hunters, similar to the ocean turtles, can profit from the accessibility of jellyfish as a food source, the modified energy elements might influence different parts of the food web, prompting flowing impacts.

The Jellyfish-Environment Input Circle

Jellyfish blossoms and their results add to an intricate criticism circle inside marine biological systems. Natural changes, including environmental change and overfishing, can set off jellyfish sprouts, which, thusly, impact the overflow and dispersion of different species. Understanding the instruments of this input circle is urgent for anticipating and dealing with the biological effects of jellyfish elements.

Connections with Fish Populaces

Fisheries Effect: Disturbance and Financial Outcomes

The connections among jellyfish and fish populaces stretch out past environmental elements to incorporate huge financial and cultural ramifications. In locales where jellyfish blossoms disturb fisheries, the results can be significant, influencing the jobs of anglers and the maintainability of fisheries assets.

Harm to Fishing Stuff:

Jellyfish blossoms can disrupt fishing exercises by harming stuff like nets and fishes. The thick bodies and limbs of jellyfish might become snared in fishing hardware, prompting diminished get quality and functional difficulties for anglers.

Contest for Assets:

The opposition among jellyfish and fish for food assets can influence fisheries by lessening the accessibility of key prey things for economically significant fish species. This opposition further features the requirement for feasible fisheries the board rehearses that think about the more extensive biological system elements.

Overfishing and Trophic Interruption

Overfishing, driven by human interest for fish, can add to trophic disturbance and the expansion of jellyfish in marine environments. The expulsion of specific fish species through overfishing can deliver predation strain on jellyfish, permitting their populaces to flood.

Undermining Food Networks:

The consumption of fish populaces due to overfishing can weaken marine food networks, making uneven characters that favor jellyfish. As jellyfish populaces increment, they may outcompete or go after fish hatchlings and little fish, intensifying the difficulties looked by fisheries.

Changes in Species Structure:

Overfishing-actuated trophic disturbance might prompt changes in the species sythesis of marine biological systems. The downfall of monetarily significant fish species and the ascent of jellyfish can modify the construction and elements of environments, impacting the versatility and maintainability of fisheries.

Seaside Biological systems: The travel industry and Human Communications

Influence on The travel industry

Jellyfish associations with people likewise happen with regards to the travel industry and diversion. A few types of jellyfish have stinging cells that can make distress or injury people. The presence of jellyfish blossoms close to beach front regions can present difficulties for the travel industry, with possible ramifications for neighborhood economies.

Security Concerns:

Jellyfish stings can go from gentle distress to extreme responses, contingent upon the species and the singular's responsiveness. In regions where jellyfish sprouts are normal, wellbeing concerns might emerge, provoking ocean side terminations and affecting sporting exercises.

Monetary Outcomes:

The monetary outcomes of jellyfish stings and their effect on the travel industry can be significant. Seaside people group that depend on the travel industry income might confront difficulties when jellyfish blossoms influence guest wellbeing and the general the travel industry experience.

Human-Jellyfish Associations

The associations among people and jellyfish stretch out past security worries to incorporate logical exploration, training, and the social meaning of these thick creatures.

Logical Investigation:

Jellyfish give significant open doors to logical investigation and examination. Concentrating on their science, conduct, and environmental associations adds to how we might interpret marine biological systems and the more extensive ramifications of jellyfish elements.

Instructive Effort:

Instructive effort projects can assume a significant part in cultivating public mindfulness and comprehension of jellyfish. By giving data about jellyfish science, their environmental job, and security measures, networks can more readily explore human-jellyfish cooperations.

Social Importance:

Jellyfish hold social importance in specific social orders, highlighting in fantasies, fables, and creative articulations. Investigating the social elements of human-jellyfish associations adds extravagance to our enthusiasm for these puzzling animals.

Preservation Suggestions and The board Methodologies

Adjusting Preservation and Asset Use

Preserving marine environments while tending to the difficulties presented by jellyfish elements requires a reasonable methodology that considers biological flexibility, feasible asset use, and the necessities of beach front networks.

Supportable Fisheries The board:

Carrying out supportable fisheries the board rehearses is fundamental for moderating the effect of jellyfish on fisheries and keeping up with the soundness of marine biological systems. This incorporates setting get limits, safeguarding basic territories, and staying away from overfishing that can add to trophic disturbance.

Biological system Based Administration:

Embracing environment based administration approaches recognizes the interconnected idea of marine biological systems. Taking into account the job of jellyfish inside the more extensive setting of environment elements considers more all encompassing protection techniques that address the intricacies of trophic connections.

Observing and Early Admonition Frameworks

Creating observing projects and early admonition frameworks for jellyfish sprouts empowers proactive reactions to their environmental and financial outcomes.

Remote Detecting Innovations:

Using remote detecting innovations, like satellite symbolism and submerged advanced mechanics, takes into account constant checking of jellyfish populaces and their natural triggers. Early recognition gives a chance to carry out administration measures before blossoms raise.

Coordinated Information Stages:

Coordinating information from different sources, including natural observing, environment information, and fisheries evaluations, makes far reaching stages for grasping jellyfish elements. This coordinated methodology upgrades the ability to foresee and answer changes in marine biological systems.

Public Mindfulness and Schooling

Raising public mindfulness and instructing networks about jellyfish science, security measures, and the more extensive natural setting encourages a feeling of obligation and stewardship.

Instructive Missions:

Instructive missions can disperse data about jellyfish, their job in marine environments, and security rules for connecting with them. Joint efforts between researchers, policymakers, and nearby networks add to informed navigation.

Resident Science Drives:

Drawing in people in general in resident science drives considers the assortment of important information on jellyfish events. Resident researchers can contribute perceptions, helping scientists in grasping the conveyance and overflow of jellyfish in various areas.

Environmental Change Moderation

Tending to the underlying drivers of environmental change, including the decrease of ozone harming substance emanations, is significant for alleviating the effect of ecological changes on jellyfish elements.

Economical Practices:

Advancing economical practices at individual, local area, and modern levels adds to environmental change alleviation. Endeavors to diminish fossil fuel byproducts, safeguard seaside living spaces, and change to sustainable power sources are fundamental parts of a far reaching technique.

Variation Systems:

Creating variation systems that record for the effects of environmental change on marine environments improves the flexibility of seaside networks. Versatile measures can incorporate the reclamation of beach front environments, reasonable hydroponics practices, and local area based protection drives.

Future Exploration Headings

Jellyfish Nature and Conduct

Progressions in understanding jellyfish environment and conduct offer promising roads for future exploration. Investigating the elements that impact jellyfish developments, taking care of ways of behaving, and conceptive techniques adds to a more nuanced comprehension of their part in marine biological systems.

Social Biology:

Exploring the social biology of jellyfish, including their reactions to ecological signals, hunter aversion procedures, and communications with different species, gives experiences into the elements of their developments and circulation.

Regenerative Science:

Concentrating on the conceptive science of jellyfish improves our insight into their life history systems. Research on conceptive cycles, larval turn of events, and the elements impacting regenerative achievement adds to how we might interpret jellyfish populace elements.

Atomic Experiences into Jellyfish Science

Progresses in sub-atomic science offer chances to dig into the hereditary and biochemical parts of jellyfish science.

Genomic Studies:

Investigating the genomes of various jellyfish species gives experiences into their transformative history, versatile qualities, and hereditary variety. Genomic studies add to how we might interpret the hereditary premise of jellyfish science.

Poison Creation Instruments:

Exploring the components fundamental poison creation in specific jellyfish species adds as far as anyone is concerned of their guarded procedures. Understanding the atomic premise of poison creation improves our capacity to anticipate and deal with the outcomes of jellyfish blossoms.

Environmental Change and Biological system Versatility

Research on the collaborations among jellyfish and marine environments with regards to environmental change is a critical region for future examination.

Environment Driven Variations:

Understanding how jellyfish and different species inside marine environments adjust to environment driven changes adds to forecasts about future natural elements. Research on versatile reactions upgrades our capacity to foster protection systems that record for the effects of environmental change.

Environment Flexibility:

Researching the versatility of marine biological systems to jellyfish elements and other ecological stressors gives bits of knowledge into the variables that add to environment soundness. Research on biological system strength adds to the advancement of procedures that improve the flexibility of marine networks.

Chapter 7

Human-Jellyfish Interactions

Competition for Resources:
In regions where jellyfish blooms coincide with key fishing grounds, competition for resources between jellyfish and commercially valuable fish species may arise. The increased predation on zooplankton by jellyfish can limit the availability of this essential food source for fish larvae and juveniles.

Sustainable Fisheries Management
Mitigating the economic impact of jellyfish on fisheries involves adopting sustainable fisheries management practices. Balancing the conservation of marine ecosystems with the sustainable use of fisheries resources is essential for the long-term viability of coastal communities.

Catch Limits and Regulation:
Implementing catch limits for both jellyfish and commercially valuable fish species helps maintain the balance of predator-prey dynamics in marine ecosystems. Regulatory measures ensure that fishing activities are conducted within sustainable limits, preventing overexploitation.

Protection of Critical Habitats:
Preserving critical habitats, including breeding and nursery areas for fish, contributes to the resilience of fish populations. Healthy ecosystems, with intact habitats, are more robust in the face of challenges posed by jellyfish blooms and other environmental stressors.

Tourism and Coastal Communities
Impact on Tourism
Jellyfish interactions with humans also manifest in the realm of tourism. Coastal areas that experience jellyfish blooms may face challenges in attracting and retaining visitors, impacting the local economy.

Safety Concerns for Tourists:
Jellyfish stings can pose safety concerns for tourists, affecting their experience

and enjoyment of coastal destinations. Instances of jellyfish stings, particularly if not properly managed, may lead to negative reviews and decreased tourism.

Economic Consequences:

The economic consequences of jellyfish blooms on tourism can be substantial. Coastal communities that rely on tourism revenue may experience downturns if jellyfish-related safety concerns deter visitors from engaging in recreational activities.

Adaptive Tourism Practices

Adopting adaptive tourism practices can help coastal communities navigate the challenges posed by jellyfish dynamics. Proactive measures and strategies enhance the safety of tourists while supporting sustainable tourism.

Monitoring and Early Warning Systems:

Implementing monitoring programs and early warning systems allows coastal communities to anticipate and respond to jellyfish blooms. Providing timely information to tourists enables them to make informed decisions about their activities.

Safety Measures and Outreach:

Educational outreach programs inform tourists about jellyfish biology, safety measures, and first aid procedures. Equipping tourists with knowledge empowers them to enjoy coastal environments responsibly and safely.

Cultural Perspectives on Jellyfish

Jellyfish hold cultural significance in various societies, contributing to the diversity of perspectives on these gelatinous creatures.

Symbolism in Art and Myth:

In some cultures, jellyfish symbolize adaptability, mystery, and the ever-changing nature of the sea. Artists draw inspiration from these symbolic meanings, incorporating jellyfish into artistic expressions that reflect the deep connections between humans and the marine environment.

Rituals and Festivals:

Certain communities celebrate jellyfish through rituals and festivals. These events often highlight the cultural importance of marine life, fostering a sense of connection between local populations and the ocean.

Scientific Outreach and Education

Scientific outreach and education initiatives bridge the gap between scientific knowledge and public understanding, fostering an appreciation for jellyfish and marine ecosystems.

Public Lectures and Workshops:

Scientists and marine biologists engage with the public through lectures and workshops, sharing their expertise on jellyfish biology, ecology, and conservation. These events contribute to a broader understanding of marine science and its relevance to everyday life.

Children's Programs:

Educational programs targeting children play a crucial role in shaping future perspectives on marine conservation. Hands-on activities, interactive exhibits, and outreach initiatives inspire a sense of wonder and curiosity about the marine world.

Conservation Implications and Future Perspectives

Ecosystem-Based Conservation

Conserving marine ecosystems requires an ecosystem-based approach that considers the interconnectedness of species and the complex dynamics that shape marine environments.

Holistic Conservation Strategies:

Ecosystem-based conservation strategies acknowledge the interactions between jellyfish, fish, and other components of marine ecosystems. By considering the broader ecological context, these strategies aim to promote resilience and sustainability.

Adaptive Management:

Adaptive management approaches involve continuously learning from ecosystem responses and adjusting conservation strategies accordingly. Flexibility in conservation measures allows for effective responses to changing environmental conditions, including jellyfish dynamics.

Climate Change and Adaptation

Addressing the impacts of climate change is essential for the long-term resilience of marine ecosystems and the species that inhabit them.

Mitigating Climate Change:

Reducing greenhouse gas emissions and mitigating the effects of climate change are critical components of preserving marine biodiversity. Global efforts to transition to renewable energy sources, protect carbon sinks, and promote sustainable practices contribute to climate change mitigation.

Adaptation Strategies:

Coastal communities and ecosystems must adapt to the changing climate. Implementing adaptation strategies, such as habitat restoration, sustainable aquaculture practices, and community-based conservation initiatives, enhances the ability of marine environments to withstand stressors, including those associated with jellyfish.

Sustainable Fisheries and Coexistence

Striking a balance between sustainable fisheries and the coexistence of humans with jellyfish requires collaborative efforts and a commitment to responsible resource management.

Collaborative Research:

Collaborations between scientists, policymakers, and local communities facilitate research that informs sustainable fisheries management. Integrating traditional knowledge with scientific insights enhances the understanding of marine ecosystems.

Stakeholder Engagement:

Involving stakeholders, including fishermen, in decision-making processes fosters a sense of ownership and responsibility. Engaging with local communities ensures that conservation measures align with the needs and priorities of those directly impacted by jellyfish dynamics.

Contest for Assets:

In locales where jellyfish sprouts correspond with key fishing grounds, rivalry for assets among jellyfish and economically significant fish species might emerge. The expanded predation on zooplankton by jellyfish can restrict the accessibility of this fundamental food hotspot for fish hatchlings and adolescents.

Reasonable Fisheries The executives

Relieving the financial effect of jellyfish on fisheries includes taking on economical fisheries the executives rehearses. Adjusting the preservation of marine environments with the supportable utilization of fisheries assets is fundamental for the drawn out feasibility of waterfront networks.

Get Cutoff points and Guideline:

Carrying out get limits for both jellyfish and financially significant fish species keeps up with the equilibrium of hunter prey elements in marine biological systems. Administrative measures guarantee that fishing exercises are directed inside supportable cutoff points, forestalling overexploitation.

Insurance of Basic Living spaces:

Saving basic living spaces, including rearing and nursery regions for fish, adds to the versatility of fish populaces. Solid biological systems, with flawless living spaces, are more strong despite challenges presented by jellyfish sprouts and other ecological stressors.

The travel industry and Seaside People group

Influence on The travel industry

Jellyfish cooperations with people additionally manifest in the domain of the travel industry. Seaside regions that experience jellyfish blossoms might confront difficulties in drawing in and holding guests, affecting the nearby economy.

Security Worries for Sightseers:

Jellyfish stings can present security worries for sightseers, influencing their experience and happiness regarding waterfront objections. Occurrences of jellyfish stings, especially while possibly not appropriately made due, may prompt negative audits and diminished the travel industry.

Monetary Outcomes:

The financial results of jellyfish blossoms on the travel industry can be significant. Beach front networks that depend on the travel industry income might encounter slumps if jellyfish-related security concerns hinder guests from participating in sporting exercises.

Versatile The travel industry Practices

Taking on versatile the travel industry practices can assist beach front networks with exploring the difficulties presented by jellyfish elements. Proactive measures and systems improve the security of travelers while supporting practical the travel industry.

Checking and Early Admonition Frameworks:

Carrying out checking programs and early admonition frameworks permits beach front networks to expect and answer jellyfish sprouts. Giving opportune data to travelers empowers them to settle on informed conclusions about their exercises.

Wellbeing Measures and Effort:

Instructive effort programs illuminate sightseers about jellyfish science, security measures, and emergency treatment strategies. Outfitting travelers with information enables them to appreciate seaside conditions capably and securely.

Social Points of view on Jellyfish

Jellyfish hold social importance in different social orders, adding to the variety of points of view on these coagulated animals.

Imagery in Craftsmanship and Legend:

In certain societies, jellyfish represent versatility, secret, and the steadily changing nature of the ocean. Craftsmen draw motivation from these emblematic implications, integrating jellyfish into creative articulations that mirror the profound associations among people and the marine climate.

Customs and Celebrations:

Certain people group celebrate jellyfish through ceremonies and celebrations. These occasions frequently feature the social significance of marine life, encouraging a feeling of association between nearby populaces and the sea.

Logical Effort and Instruction

Logical effort and instruction drives overcome any barrier between logical information and public grasping, encouraging an appreciation for jellyfish and marine environments.

Public Talks and Studios:

Researchers and sea life scientists draw in with people in general through talks and studios, sharing their aptitude on jellyfish science, environment, and protection. These occasions add to a more extensive comprehension of sea life science and its significance to day to day existence.

Kids' Projects:

Instructive projects focusing on kids assume a pivotal part in molding future points of view on marine preservation. Involved exercises, intelligent displays, and effort drives move a feeling of marvel and interest in the marine world.

Preservation Suggestions and Future Points of view

Environment Based Preservation

Moderating marine biological systems requires an environment based approach that thinks about the interconnectedness of species and the complicated elements that shape marine conditions.

Comprehensive Protection Systems:

Biological system based protection procedures recognize the cooperations between jellyfish, fish, and different parts of marine environments. By taking into account the more extensive natural setting, these systems mean to advance strength and manageability.

Versatile Administration:

Versatile administration approaches include ceaselessly gaining from biological system reactions and changing preservation techniques appropriately. Adaptability in preservation measures considers successful reactions to changing natural circumstances, including jellyfish elements.

Environmental Change and Transformation

Tending to the effects of environmental change is fundamental for the drawn out strength of marine biological systems and the species that occupy them.

Moderating Environmental Change:

Diminishing ozone depleting substance emanations and moderating the impacts of environmental change are basic parts of protecting marine biodiversity. Worldwide endeavors to progress to environmentally friendly power sources, safeguard carbon sinks, and elevate supportable practices add to environmental change alleviation.

Transformation Systems:

Waterfront people group and biological systems should adjust to the evolving environment. Executing variation methodologies, for example, territory rebuilding, manageable hydroponics practices, and local area based preservation drives, upgrades the capacity of marine conditions to endure stressors, incorporating those related with jellyfish.

Economical Fisheries and Conjunction

Finding some kind of harmony between economical fisheries and the conjunction of people with jellyfish requires cooperative endeavors and a promise to dependable asset the executives.

Cooperative Exploration:

Joint efforts between researchers, policymakers, and neighborhood networks work with research that illuminates maintainable fisheries the board. Coordinating conventional information with logical bits of knowledge improves the comprehension of marine environments.

Partner Commitment:

Including partners, including anglers, in dynamic cycles cultivates a feeling of pride and obligation. Drawing in with nearby networks guarantees that preservation measures line up with the requirements and needs of those straightforwardly affected by jellyfish elements.

7.1 Stinging Incidents and First Aid Measures

Jellyfish, with their smooth developments and ethereal appearance, are enamoring animals possessing marine conditions across the globe. While these thick creatures add to the mind boggling embroidery of sea life, a few animal varieties have stinging cells that can cause uneasiness, torment, and, at times, represent a danger to human wellbeing. This investigation digs into stinging occurrences brought about by jellyfish experiences and the fundamental emergency treatment measures to explore the repercussions.

The Instrument of Jellyfish Stings

Jellyfish stings result from the release of specific cells called nematocysts, which are situated on the appendages of these marine animals. Nematocysts contain a wound, string like construction that, upon contact with the skin, quickly spreads out and infuses toxin into the person in question. The piece of the toxin differs among jellyfish species, adding to the assorted scope of responses saw in people following stings.

Separating Between Jellyfish Stings

Different types of jellyfish are tracked down in seas, oceans, and beach front waters, each with its own arrangement of qualities and likely effect on people. Separating between jellyfish stings is critical for giving proper medical aid and clinical therapy.

Box Jellyfish:

Box jellyfish, found fundamentally in the Indo-Pacific locale, are known for their powerful toxin. Stings from enclose jellyfish can result serious agony, cardiovascular complexities, and, in outrageous cases, fatalities. Recognizable proof of box jellyfish and brief clinical consideration are basic while experiencing this species.

Portuguese Man o' War:

While not a genuine jellyfish, the Portuguese Man o' War is much of the time experienced in sea waters. Its arms can cause excruciating stings, and the unmistakable appearance of this species, with its drifting blue or pink gas-filled bladder, supports distinguishing proof.

Normal Jellyfish Species:

Notwithstanding the more venomous species, experiences with normal jellyfish, like moon jellyfish, lion's mane jellyfish, and ocean brambles, can likewise bring about stinging episodes. While these stings are for the most part less extreme, they can in any case cause distress and limited responses.

Side effects of Jellyfish Stings

The side effects of jellyfish stings can fluctuate generally founded on elements, for example, the species in question, the singular's awareness, and the degree of contact. Normal side effects include:

Agony and Uneasiness:

Prompt agony and inconvenience at the site of the sting are run of the mill responses. The seriousness of agony can go from gentle to extraordinary, contingent upon the species and how much toxin conveyed.

Redness and Enlarging:

The impacted region might show redness and enlarging, demonstrating an incendiary reaction to the toxin. This restricted response is a typical part of jellyfish stings.

Tingling and Aggravation:

Tingling and aggravation might go with the sting site, adding to the general inconvenience experienced by the person. Scratching the impacted region can worsen side effects.

Rash and Hives:

At times, jellyfish stings might bring about the improvement of a rash or hives on the skin encompassing the sting site. This is many times part of the fiery reaction.

Foundational Responses:

Serious jellyfish stings, especially those from exceptionally venomous species, can prompt fundamental responses. These may incorporate sickness, heaving, muscle cramps, trouble breathing, and, in outrageous cases, cardiovascular breakdown.

Medical aid Measures for Jellyfish Stings

Speedy and proper emergency treatment measures are vital for lightening side effects, forestalling confusions, and giving help to people who have encountered jelly-fish stings. The particular emergency treatment steps can shift in view of the kind of jellyfish included, yet a few overall rules apply to numerous circumstances.

Escape the Water

In case of a jellyfish sting, the primary goal is to eliminate the person from the water to forestall further openness to jellyfish limbs and expected extra stings.

Don't Rub the Impacted Region

Scouring the sting site can animate the release of extra nematocysts and intensify the spread of toxin. It is urgent to try not to rub the impacted region, despite the fact that the natural response might be to reduce the aggravation.

Wash with Vinegar (for specific species)

For stings from box jellyfish and a few different animal categories, washing the impacted region with vinegar is suggested. Vinegar can help inactivate nematocysts that poor person yet delivered toxin, forestalling further envenomation.

Eliminate Limbs

Cautiously eliminating any limbs that are as yet connected to the skin is a funda-mental stage. This should be possible utilizing tweezers or the edge of a Mastercard. It means quite a bit to wear gloves or utilize a material to stay away from direct contact with the limbs.

Submerge in Steaming hot Water

For stings from specific species, like box jellyfish, submerging the impacted region in steaming hot water can assist with mitigating torment. The water ought to be serenely warm however not burning. This action isn't suggested for stings from all jellyfish species.

Use Seawater, Not Freshwater

Washing the sting site with seawater is desirable over utilizing freshwater, as fresh-water can set off the release of nematocysts. In the event that vinegar isn't accessible, seawater can be utilized for starting washing.

Take Agony Drug

Over-the-counter agony medicine, like acetaminophen or ibuprofen, can be taken to assist with overseeing torment and diminish aggravation. Allergy medicines may likewise be utilized to reduce tingling.

Look for Clinical Consideration

In instances of extreme responses, unfavorably susceptible reactions, or stings from exceptionally venomous species, it is urgent to look for sure fire clinical consideration. Clinical experts can manage suitable medicines, for example, counter-agent, relief from discomfort, and different intercessions.

Watch for Indications of Hypersensitivity

Hypersensitivity is an extreme, dangerous unfavorably susceptible response that can happen in light of jellyfish toxin. Indications of hypersensitivity incorporate trouble breathing, expanding of the face and throat, a quick or powerless heartbeat, and a drop in pulse. Assuming that these side effects happen, crisis clinical help is required.

Protection Measures and Security Tips

Forestalling jellyfish stings is a vital part of guaranteeing wellbeing in marine conditions. While experiences with jellyfish are not actually avoidable, a few precaution measures and security tips can decrease the gamble of stings.

Be Educated about Nearby Jellyfish Species

Understanding the sorts of jellyfish present in a specific locale and their qualities is fundamental for informed direction. Nearby specialists and signage at sea shores frequently give data about common jellyfish species and security safeguards.

Utilize Defensive Attire

Wearing defensive apparel, for example, wetsuits or rash gatekeepers, can decrease the gamble of jellyfish stings. These pieces of clothing give an actual obstruction between the skin and jellyfish limbs.

Remain Informed about Ocean side Circumstances

Prior to wandering into the water, it is fitting to remain informed about ocean side circumstances and any admonitions or warnings connected with jellyfish sprouts. Checking nearby climate and tide conditions can likewise add to somewhere safe and secure.

Swim in Assigned Regions

Deciding to swim in assigned swimming regions, where the water is routinely checked, can decrease the gamble of experiencing jellyfish. These regions are frequently watched by lifeguards who can give help with instance of crises.

Try not to Contact Abandoned Jellyfish

Indeed, even jellyfish that seem abandoned or washed aground may in any case have dynamic nematocysts. It is significant to try not to contact abandoned jellyfish, as this can prompt stings.

Convey Emergency treatment Supplies

Having a fundamental emergency treatment unit, including vinegar, tweezers, and torment medicine, can be significant for tending to jellyfish stings quickly. People who know about their defenselessness to jellyfish stings might consider conveying individual defensive hardware.

Be Careful during Jellyfish Blossoms

During times of jellyfish sprouts, when there is an expanded centralization of jellyfish in a specific region, additional wariness is fitting. Remaining careful and complying with wellbeing rules turns out to be considerably more basic.

7.2 Economic and Ecological Impacts of Jellyfish Blooms

Jellyfish, with their clear bodies and musical developments, add to the mind boggling trap of marine biological systems. Be that as it may, the peculiarity of jellyfish sprouts, where huge quantities of jellyfish gather in a specific region, can have broad outcomes on both the monetary exercises of waterfront networks and the natural equilibrium of marine conditions. This investigation dives into the double effects of jellyfish blossoms, revealing insight into the financial difficulties looked by fisheries and the travel industry enterprises while likewise analyzing the more extensive environmental ramifications.

Financial Effects: Difficulties for Fisheries

Gear Harm and Functional Disturbances

One of the essential financial difficulties related with jellyfish blossoms is the harm caused to fishing gear. The thick bodies and long appendages of jellyfish can catch in fishing nets, fishes, and lines, prompting functional disturbances and expanded support costs for anglers. The requirement for continuous stuff fixes decreases the effectiveness of fishing tasks and represents a monetary weight on fishing networks.

Rivalry for Assets

Jellyfish are insatiable hunters of zooplankton, a urgent food hotspot for some monetarily important fish species. During jellyfish sprouts, the expanded predation on zooplankton can disturb the equilibrium of the marine food web. This opposition for assets among jellyfish and fish hatchlings can adversely influence fish populaces, possibly prompting diminished fishery yields.

Influence on Fishery Efficiency

The presence of jellyfish in fishing grounds can bring about diminished fishery efficiency. As jellyfish populaces increment, they may outcompete fish for accessible prey, prompting decreased endurance paces of fish hatchlings and adolescents. This opposition can have flowing consequences for fish populaces, affecting the general wellbeing and maintainability of fisheries.

The travel Industry Difficulties

Wellbeing Worries for Vacationers

Jellyfish blossoms can have critical repercussions for waterfront the travel industry. Wellbeing concerns connected with jellyfish stings represent a danger to the general the travel industry experience. Travelers might be reluctant to take part in water-based exercises, affecting the income created by seaside organizations, including lodgings, cafés, and visit administrators.

Negative Insights and Public Picture

Examples of jellyfish stings and the presence of jellyfish in seaside waters can make negative discernments among expected sightseers. Negative surveys and reports of security issues can spread rapidly, deterring people from picking explicit locations for their excursions. The monetary results reach out past prompt misfortunes, influencing the drawn out standing of waterfront regions.

Decrease in Sporting Exercises

Jellyfish blossoms can prompt limitations on sporting exercises, like swimming and swimming, in impacted regions. The travel industry subordinate networks might encounter decreases in guest numbers and a comparing decrease in income from sporting administrations.

Biological Effects: Interruption of Marine Environments

Trophic Fountains

Jellyfish blossoms can set off trophic fountains, upsetting the mind boggling equilibrium of marine biological systems. The expanded predation on zooplankton by jellyfish can prompt a decrease in the wealth of these little organic entities. As zooplankton populaces decline, the creatures that feed on them, including fish hatchlings, face food deficiencies, possibly affecting the whole marine food web.

Changes in Fishery Structure

The opposition among jellyfish and fish for zooplankton can bring about shifts in the structure of fishery species. Some fish species might decrease in overflow, while others that are less reliant upon zooplankton as a food source might turn out to be more common. These progressions can have complex and flowing consequences for the design and elements of marine networks.

Oxygen Exhaustion and No man's lands

Jellyfish sprouts can add to oxygen consumption in marine conditions. As jellyfish consume zooplankton and other little living beings, they discharge natural matter that, when deteriorated by microorganisms, consumes oxygen. In regions where jellyfish sprouts are broad, the blend of oxygen consumption and the decay of natural matter can make hypoxic or anoxic circumstances, prompting the arrangement of "no man's lands" where marine life battles to get by.

Moderation and Variation Systems

Economical Fisheries The executives

Executing supportable fisheries the board rehearses is fundamental for relieving the effect of jellyfish sprouts on fisheries. This incorporates setting get limits, safeguarding basic natural surroundings, and embracing measures to diminish overfishing. By guaranteeing the versatility of fish populaces, fisheries can more readily endure the difficulties presented by jellyfish elements.

Biological system Based Administration

Taking on environment based administration approaches recognizes the interconnected idea of marine biological systems. Taking into account the job of jellyfish inside the more extensive setting of environment elements considers more all encompassing protection procedures. Adjusting the requirements of fisheries with the conservation of environment wellbeing is significant for practical asset use.

Checking and Early Admonition Frameworks

Creating checking programs and early admonition frameworks for jellyfish sprouts empowers proactive reactions to their natural and financial outcomes. Remote detecting advances, like satellite symbolism and submerged mechanical technology, take into consideration continuous observing of jellyfish populaces and their natural triggers. Early recognition gives a valuable chance to execute the board measures before sprouts heighten.

Manageable The travel industry Practices

Waterfront people group can take on supportable the travel industry practices to relieve the financial effect of jellyfish blossoms. This incorporates furnishing sightseers with data about jellyfish wellbeing, executing instructive missions, and laying out rules for dependable collaborations with marine conditions. Proactive measures, like the utilization of observing frameworks, can improve the wellbeing of vacationers and add to a positive the travel industry experience.

Environmental Change Moderation

Tending to the underlying drivers of environmental change, including the decrease of ozone depleting substance outflows, is essential for relieving the effect of ecological changes on jellyfish elements. Advancing reasonable practices at individual, local area, and modern levels adds to environmental change alleviation. Endeavors to diminish fossil fuel byproducts, safeguard waterfront territories, and change to environmentally friendly power sources are fundamental parts of a far reaching system.

7.3 Mitigation and Management Strategies

Jellyfish blossoms, portrayed by the fast expansion of jellyfish populaces, present complex difficulties for marine biological systems and the networks reliant upon them. Moderating the effects of jellyfish blossoms requires a diverse methodology that joins logical comprehension, feasible administration practices, and local area commitment. This investigation digs into the assorted techniques utilized for the alleviation and the board of jellyfish blossoms, including natural preservation, maintainable fisheries the executives, mechanical developments, and local area based drives.

Understanding the Drivers of Jellyfish Sprouts

Ecological Variables

Jellyfish sprouts are impacted by a mix of ecological elements, including ocean temperature, supplement accessibility, and sea flows. Understanding the drivers of jellyfish populace elements is central to creating powerful alleviation systems.

Temperature and Environment:

Hotter ocean temperatures, frequently connected with environmental change, can lean toward the multiplication and development of jellyfish. Checking temperature varieties and surveying their effect on jellyfish overflow add to early advance notice frameworks and versatile administration.

Supplement Levels:

Raised supplement levels, coming about because of horticultural overflow or other anthropogenic exercises, can advance the development of phytoplankton, a vital part of jellyfish slims down. Overseeing supplement contributions to waterfront waters is urgent for forestalling inordinate jellyfish expansion.

Sea Flows:

Sea flows impact the dispersion and transport of jellyfish hatchlings. Understanding the examples of sea flows predicts the development of jellyfish populaces and illuminates systems for checking and the board.

Natural Protection Methodologies

Biological system Based Administration

Taking on an environment based administration (EBM) approach perceives the interconnectedness of species inside marine biological systems. EBM thinks about the jobs of jellyfish, fish, and different living beings with regards to more extensive biological elements.

Comprehensive Protection:

Comprehensive protection systems center around safeguarding the general well-being and strength of marine environments. Safeguarding basic natural surroundings, keeping up with biodiversity, and limiting anthropogenic unsettling influences add to the steadiness of environments.

Versatile Administration:

Versatile administration includes consistent learning and change of preservation methodologies in view of progressing observing and research. Adaptability in administration rehearses considers opportune reactions to changes in jellyfish elements and natural circumstances.

Saving Normal Hunters

Recognizing and saving regular hunters of jellyfish can assist with controlling their populaces. Certain types of fish, ocean anemones, and ocean turtles are known to benefit from jellyfish. Safeguarding these hunters and their territories upholds a characteristic equilibrium in marine biological systems.

Protection of Ocean Turtles:

Ocean turtles, especially species like the leatherback turtle, feed on jellyfish and add to their control. Preservation endeavors zeroed in on safeguarding ocean turtle settling destinations and decreasing dangers, for example, bycatch upgrade their part in jellyfish populace guideline.

Advancing Fish Biodiversity:

Keeping a different fish local area is fundamental for managing jellyfish populaces. Overfishing and territory corruption can diminish fish biodiversity, possibly prompting expanded jellyfish predominance. Feasible fisheries the board rehearses assist with safeguarding fish populaces and their biological jobs.

Reasonable Fisheries The board

Get Cutoff points and Guideline

Carrying out get limits for both jellyfish and financially important fish species is fundamental for keeping an equilibrium in marine environments. Administrative measures guarantee that fishing exercises are led inside reasonable cutoff points, forestalling overexploitation of fisheries assets.

Jellyfish Collecting:

In certain locales, the deliberate gathering of jellyfish for business designs is rehearsed. Laying out get limits for jellyfish reaping forestalls inordinate expulsion, taking into consideration their natural capabilities to be kept up with.

Adjusting Predation:

Reasonable fisheries the board means to figure out some kind of harmony between fishing exercises and the regular predation of jellyfish by fish species. By directing fishing rehearses, specialists can limit the effect on fish populaces and their capacity to control jellyfish overflow.

Security of Basic Environments

Safeguarding basic environments, for example, producing and nursery regions for fish, is essential for keeping up with solid fish populaces and forestalling the expansion of jellyfish. Living space corruption can upset the existence patterns of both fish and jellyfish, prompting uneven characters in the biological system.

Marine Safeguarded Regions:

Laying out marine safeguarded regions (MPAs) helps defend basic environments and permits marine biological systems to recuperate and flourish. MPAs add to the preservation of biodiversity, support fish populaces, and advance the versatility of marine conditions.

Living space Rebuilding:

Endeavors to reestablish debased living spaces, like seagrasses and coral reefs, add to the general strength of marine biological systems. Solid territories offer fundamental types of assistance for fish populaces and improve their ability to control jellyfish.

Mechanical Advancements

Early Admonition Frameworks

Growing early admonition frameworks for jellyfish sprouts includes the utilization of cutting edge innovations to screen ecological circumstances and jellyfish populaces. These frameworks give convenient data to versatile administration and assist with alleviating the effect of sprouts.

Remote Detecting Advancements:

Satellite symbolism and remote detecting innovations empower the checking of sea conditions for an enormous scope. These apparatuses permit researchers to recognize changes in ocean surface temperature, supplement levels, and chlorophyll fixations, giving bits of knowledge into potential jellyfish blossom triggers.

Submerged Advanced mechanics:

Submerged advanced mechanics, including independent submerged vehicles (AUVs) and remotely worked vehicles (ROVs), work with the assortment of information from underneath the sea's surface. These advancements improve the accuracy and productivity of checking endeavors in regions inclined to jellyfish blossoms.

Biocontrol Measures

Investigating biocontrol measures includes distinguishing and using regular natural specialists that can assist with controlling jellyfish populaces. Research in this space plans to track down imaginative and naturally supportable arrangements.

Jellyfish Hunters:

Examining the presentation or improvement of normal jellyfish hunters might offer a biocontrol system. Recognizing living beings that specifically go after jellyfish without really hurting other marine life is a complex yet possibly powerful road for control.

Hereditary Adjustment:

Investigation into hereditary change procedures looks to foster kinds of fish or different creatures with an expanded craving for jellyfish. While disputable, these methodologies present opportunities for focused on and harmless to the ecosystem control measures.

Local area Based Drives

Public Mindfulness and Instruction

Connecting with neighborhood networks and the overall population in jellyfish mindfulness and schooling drives is critical for cultivating a feeling of obligation and understanding. Public mindfulness crusades give data on jellyfish biology, security measures, and the significance of economical practices.

Resident Science Projects:

Including the general population in jellyfish checking through resident science programs contributes important information to logical examination. Empowering people to report jellyfish sightings and partake in information assortment improves the comprehension of jellyfish elements.

Instructive Effort:

Instructive projects in schools, public venues, and beach front regions bring issues to light about the environmental jobs of jellyfish, wellbeing measures, and the interconnectedness of marine biological systems. Informed people group are bound to take part in preservation endeavors effectively.

Supportable The travel industry Practices

Taking on feasible the travel industry rehearses adds to the capable administration of beach front regions and lessens the effect of the travel industry related exercises on jellyfish populaces.

Vacationer Schooling:

Instructing vacationers about jellyfish security, capable way of behaving, and the significance of marine protection cultivates a feeling of ecological stewardship. Vacationer schooling projects can be executed through educational materials, directed visits, and effort drives.

Checking and Detailing Frameworks:

Laying out checking and detailing frameworks for jellyfish sightings in famous vacationer locations considers the convenient dispersal of data. Sightseers can come to informed conclusions about water-based exercises, lessening the gamble of stings and advancing a positive the travel industry experience.